INSPIRATION
IN
CROSS STITCH

DOROTHEA HALL

INSPIRATION
IN
CROSS STITCH

40 Gifts and Keepsakes for Christian Celebrations

DOROTHEA HALL

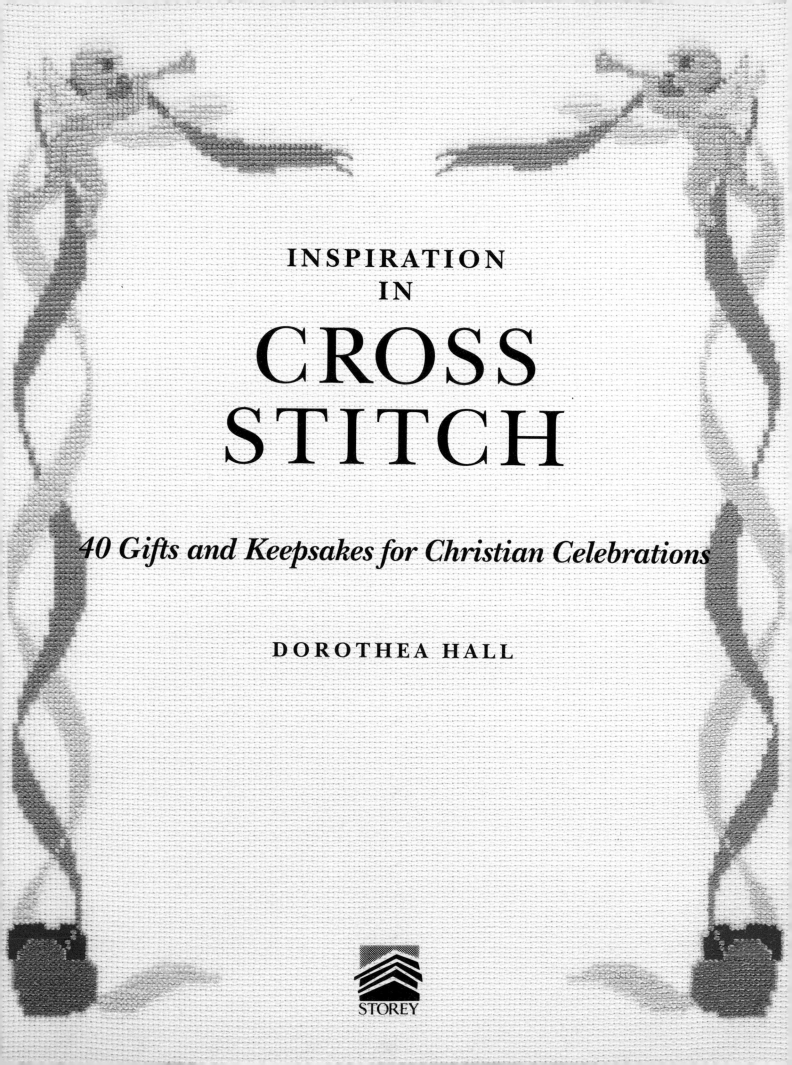

STOREY

To the memory of my parents.

United States edition published in 1995 by Storey Communications, Inc.,
Schoolhouse Road, Pownal, Vermont 05261
First Published in the UK in 1994 by
New Holland (Publishers) Ltd
37 Connaught Street, London W2 2AZ

ISBN 0-88266-851-X

Editorial direction: Yvonne McFarlane
Editor: Felicity Jackson
Storey Communications editor: Gwen W. Steege
Designer: Roger Daniels
Storey Communications designer: Michelle Arabia
Photographer: Jon Stewart
Stylist: Barbara Stewart
Alphabet charts: Chris Mullen
Line illustrations and charts: Julie Ward
Step-by-step illustrations: King and King
Design styling: Peter Bridgewater

The Chess Players, courtesy The Bridgeman Art Library, page 136.

Typeset by Textype Typesetters. Reproduction by Modern Age Repro House,
Hong Kong. Printed and bound in Malaysia by Times Offset (M) SDN BHD.

Library of Congress Cataloging-in-Publication Data

Hall, Dorothea.
    Inspiration in cross stitch : 40 heirloom gifts and keepsakes /
Dorothea Hall.
        p.   cm.
    "A Storey Publishing book."
    Includes bibliographical references and index.
    ISBN 0-88266-851-X (hc)
TT178.C76H349   1995
746.44'3041–dc20   95-123
                                                                  CIP

CONTENTS

I N T R O D U C T I O N

A HAND-EMBROIDERED GIFT, no matter how small, that has been carefully created and affectionately given, will always be cherished – and not least because of the emotional and personal value it embodies. It was with these thoughts in mind that *Inspiration in Cross Stitch* began.

We all have a multiplicity of relationships, and a series of events and celebrations which we like to mark by giving and exchanging gifts. Some gifts are given to celebrate birthdays and weddings, while others are simply a spontaneous response of appreciation. My aim has been to design a range of projects that would cover most of the occasions where personal gifts are appropriate, varied enough to appeal to people of all ages and tastes, so that the reader would be inspired to take up her or his sewing needle.

I have concentrated my designs on the important, happy landmarks in life, such as birthdays, christenings and weddings, where there is usually sufficient time to choose your gift and plan the making of it. For these occasions, I've designed a variety of cushions and pillows, covers, birthday cards and baby garments – each one easy to make.

Similarly, for holiday events of religious significance,

such as Easter and Christmas time, there are greeting cards, Christmas stockings and tree ornaments to make. Finally, ending on a sentimental theme, and emphasizing the very special nature of the bond between child and parent, there is a very pretty, scented sleep pillow for Mother's Day and a classic chessboard for Father's Day.

With each project design, I have tried to encapsulate the essential characteristics of the particular occasion, and also to emphasize its emotional content. It is said that, 'Affections are our life. We live by them; they supply our warmth', and, after all, when we have affection for someone, we are halfway to offering a gift.

For the cross stitch designs, my inspiration came from aspects of everyday life related to the people we love, including homes, gardens, flower garlands, family pets, religion and hobbies. I felt that these simple basics should be the essential premise for the designs but, in many cases, they could be further embellished and made quite unique by the addition of personal names, dates and appropriate mottoes.

It gives me great pleasure to think that other people will be inspired to make some of the projects in the book and, perhaps, one day I may see, for example, the little baby's first slippers with rosebuds embroidered on the soles – I did this simply because I thought that was all people could see of my own granddaughter at her christening! The scissors dolly, on the other hand, which is embroidered on both sides and represents a young girl with flowing fair hair, dressed in a long flower-sprigged dress and carrying a basket of flowers, reminded me of how much I adored my dolls as a child. I thought how charming it would be as a Mother's Day gift, or it could be given to a small child as a hand toy or pocket doll. In fact, the baby's bonnet and christening gown could easily be made for a favorite bigger doll, and consider the joy it would bring to the recipient.

I have derived enormous pleasure from designing the projects and writing the book, and I sincerely hope that the reader will be inspired to take up a needle – for what better way is there to express one's love and affection than with beautiful personalized gifts you have made yourself.

BEFORE YOU BEGIN TO EMBROIDER

⌐ MATERIALS LIST

The list of materials required, which is given with each project, states the exact measurements of fabrics, cardboard, trims and so on. However, because some evenweave fabrics fray easily, an extra 3 cm (1¼ in) all around has been included to allow for handling and stretching in a frame.

⌐ THREADS

A separate thread list for DMC 6-stranded embroidery floss is given with each chart and, unless otherwise stated in the list, you will need one skein of each color. Obviously, for small areas you will use less than a skein so it would be economical first to check if you already have odd threads of the same colors that could be used.

⌐ ORGANIZER

Once you have got your project threads together, it is a good idea to attach them to a piece of cardboard for safe keeping. You will need a piece of stiff cardboard with holes punched down one side. Cut your threads into a workable length of 50 cm (20 in) and knot them through the holes, adding their shade number opposite, in the order of the thread list.

⌐ CENTERING YOUR DESIGN

Always begin your embroidery by marking the center of your fabric both ways with tacking (basting) stitches, as indicated by the arrows on the chart. Begin stitching in the middle of the fabric, using the center lines on the chart and the tacking (basting) threads as reference points for counting the squares and fabric threads to center your design accurately.

⌐ PRESSING

Remember when pressing your finished embroidery to place it right side down on a thick, clean towel. Using a steam iron or a dry iron and damp cloth, press with up-and-down movements, to give it a well-raised effect.

CHAPTER

1

—

FOR FAMILY AND FRIENDS

Birthdays

*I count myself in nothing else so happy
As in a soul remembering my good friends.*

Richard II,
WILLIAM SHAKESPEARE

BIRTHDAY GREETING CARDS

There is nothing more pleasurable than to give and to receive flowers. Even the smallest hand-picked posy will delight the eye and instantly lift the heart. And how much greater the pleasure for friends and relatives to receive a beautifully stitched birthday posy framed in a professionally cut mount. They would be delighted with such a birthday card, then, after the day, the embroidery could be framed under glass as a keepsake picture.

Each birthday greeting card measures overall 20 cm × 14 cm (8 in × 5½ in) with cut-outs measuring 14 cm × 9.5 cm (5½ in × 3¾ in)

'Hurray! Hurrah! Many Happy Returns!' they shouted, and they hammered joyously on the tables.

The Fellowship of the Ring,

J R R TOLKEIN

MATERIALS

Dog roses card
23 cm × 18 cm (9 in × 7 in) of white Aida fabric, 13 threads to 2.5 cm (1 in)
Tacking (basting) thread
Tapestry needle size 24
Small embroidery hoop (optional)
DMC 6-stranded embroidery floss: see the appropriate thread list on page 15
17 small yellow glass beads
15 small white pearl beads
White sewing thread and small crewel needle
Card mount with landscape rectangular cut-out (see page 157 for suppliers)

Forget-me-not and ivy card
23 cm × 18 cm (9 in × 7 in) of white Aida fabric, 16 threads to 2.5 cm (1 in)
Tacking (basting) thread
Tapestry needle size 24
Small embroidery hoop (optional)
DMC 6-stranded embroidery floss: see the appropriate thread list on page 15
Card mount with upright oval cut-out (see page 157 for suppliers)

Japonica card
23 cm × 18 cm (9 in × 7 in) of pale blue Aida fabric, 16 threads to 2.5 cm (1 in)
Tacking (basting) thread
Tapestry needle size 24
Small embroidery hoop (optional)
DMC 6-stranded embroidery floss: see the appropriate thread list on page 15
76 cm (30 in) pale blue ribbon, 6 mm (¼ in) wide
Card mount with upright oval cut-out (see page 157 for suppliers)

☞ THREAD LISTS

Dog roses card

948	flesh	320	green
760	pink	895	dark green
356	brick red	725	yellow
761	pale pink	733	olive green
3778	rose pink	3776	rust
3328	deep pink	781	light brown
772	pale green	918	deep rust

Forget-me-not and ivy

445	pale yellow	211	mauve
972	orange	772	pale green
900	red	503	sage green
3747	pale blue	907	grass green
809	blue	469	sap green

Japonica

948	pale salmon pink	722	pale green
760	salmon pink	954	light viridian green
744	yellow	562	green
963	pale pink	3013	pale olive green
604	pink		
602	deep pink	731	olive green

☞ THE EMBROIDERY

In each case, mark the center of the fabric both ways with tacking (basting) stitches and work in a hoop, if preferred (see page 142). Following the appropriate color key and chart, where one square represents one cross stitch, work the embroidery using two strands of thread in the needle. Work the cross stitching first and then the backstitching on top, as shown on the chart.

For the dog rose design, complete the embroidery and then add the yellow beads to the

*I*t's my birthday. The happiest day of the year.

Winnie the Pooh,

A A MILNE

flower centers as indicated in the chart, stitching with a single strand of yellow embroidery floss (see the diagram on page 144). Using white sewing thread, attach the pearl beads in the positions indicated in the chart.

For the forget-me-not design, work the stems first, followed by the leaves and flowers and then the darker background. Next, using orange 972, add French knots to the middles of the flowers (see page 145),work the backstitching and then the lettering last of all. Steam press the embroidery on the wrong side, but leave the tacking (basting) stitches in at this stage: you will

find them helpful for centering the design in the card mount.

ASSEMBLING THE CARDS
Simply open out the self-adhesive card mount and centrally place your embroidery over the cut-out area, using the tacking (basting) as a guide. Trim the fabric so that it is 12 mm (½ in) bigger all around than the marked area on the card. Take out the tacking (basting). Reposition your embroidery, fold over the left-hand section of the card and press firmly to secure. Tie ribbon around the japonica design card to finish.

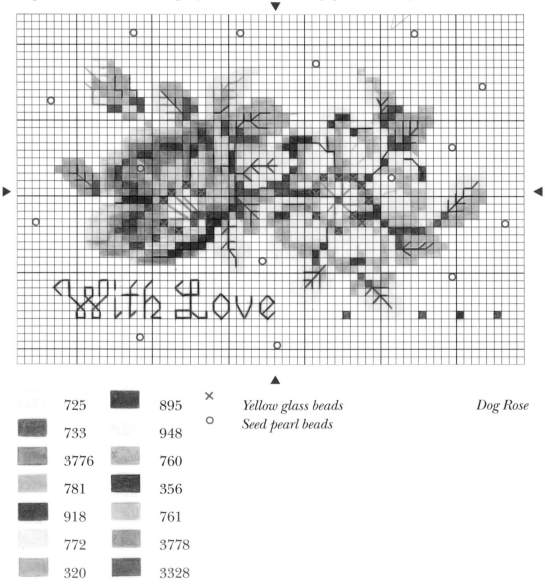

	725		895	×	Yellow glass beads		*Dog Rose*
	733		948	o	Seed pearl beads		
	3776		760				
	781		356				
	918		761				
	772		3778				
	320		3328				

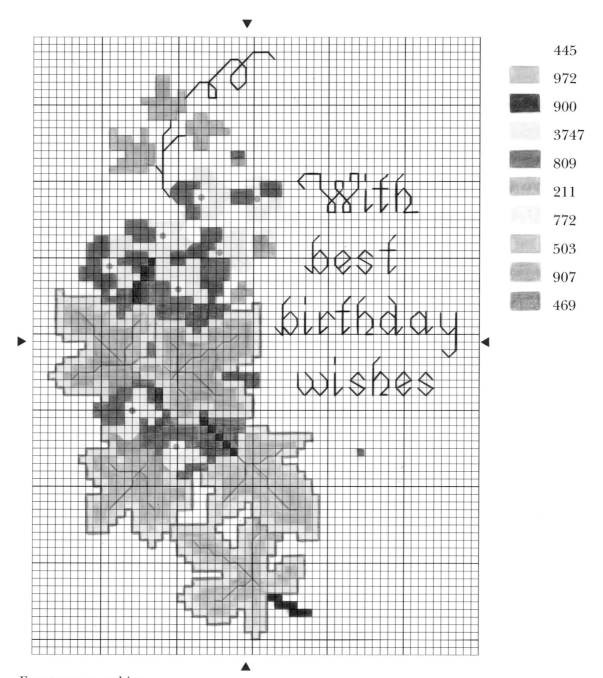

Forget-me-not and ivy

445
972
900
3747
809
211
772
503
907
469

948
760
744
963
604
602
722
954
562
3013
731

Japonica

CHILD'S PRAYER SAMPLER

In moments of reflection we are sometimes surprised by how clear and lasting are our childhood impressions. One of my earliest memories is of my sister and I, scrubbed clean and dressed in long white winceyette nightgowns, kneeling by the side of our comfy feather bed and saying aloud, to my mother, this child's prayer before jumping into bed. I wasn't always sure that I understood the last two lines, but they felt right. A similar picture to this prayer sampler hung over our bed right through our childhood until, eventually, we gave it to a baby cousin. Perhaps it is still being passed on to other little children – a comforting thought.

The finished (unframed) sampler measures
24 cm × 28 cm (9½ in × 11 in)

☞ MATERIALS
34 cm × 38 cm (13½ in × 15 in) of cream Aida
    fabric, 14 threads to 2.5 cm (1 in)
Tacking (basting) thread in a dark color
Embroidery frame (optional)
DMC 6-stranded embroidery floss: see the thread
    list below
Tapestry needle size 24
24 cm × 28 cm (9½ in × 11 in) of 3 mm (⅛ in)
    cardboard for mounting the embroidery
24 cm × 28 cm (9½ in × 11 in) of lightweight
    synthetic wadding (batting)
Strong thread or masking tape for securing the
    mounted embroidery
Picture frame of your choice

☞ THREAD LIST

725	medium yellow	562	viridian green
977	deep yellow	648	pale grey
225	pale pink	926	medium grey
3708	pink	676	soft gold
3712	medium pink	613	fawn
3013	pale grey green	640	light brown
3012	olive green	3021	dark brown
993	light viridian green	350	red

Jesus meek and mild,

pon a little child,

y simplicity,

me to come to thee.

	725
	977
	225
	3708
	3712
	3013
	3012
	993
	562
	648
	926
	676
	613
	640
	3021
	350

✎ THE EMBROIDERY

Mark the center of your fabric both ways with tacking (basting) stitches and, if you prefer, stretch it in a frame (see page 143). Following the chart and, stitching outwards from the center, begin the embroidery using two strands in the needle throughout and working one cross stitch over one woven block of fabric.

When stitching, do not carry your threads across the back of the fabric. On openweave fabrics, they may show through on the right side. They should be started and finished underneath an embroidered area. Alternatively, when more embroidery has been completed, you can neatly run your thread through the back of the stitches where it will not be seen on the front.

Half stitches are used to give greater clarity to a particular detail, such as the top of the duck's beak. Complete the cross stitching and then work the backstitching as shown on the chart. Work tiny French knots to suggest the eyes of the small birds, following the diagram on page 145.

The robin's breast and the backstitching on the duck's beak are worked in red 350. The finer tree branches are backstitched in olive green 3012.

Remove the embroidery from the frame and lightly steam-press, if needed. Do not remove the tacking (basting) threads at this stage.

Mount and frame the completed embroidery following the instructions on page 148.

❦

If there is anything that will endure
The eye of God, because it still is pure
It is the spirit of a little child,
Fresh from His hand, and therefore undefiled.

The Children's Prayer,

R H STODDARD

Christenings

There's a Friend for little children
Above the bright blue sky
A Friend who never changes,
Whose love can never die.

Children's Hymn,
ALBERT MIDLANE

CHRISTENING GOWN

A pretty first white dress is a useful and very acceptable gift for a new arrival. This dress is based on the one I made for my own children's baptism. It has the tiniest border of pink and yellow roses embroidered across the front yoke, a full skirt and short puff sleeves. To complete the ensemble for a baptism, the little jacket on page 55, would keep the baby snug and warm. Because of its simplicity as a christening gown, it would just as easily double as a special occasion dress.

The finished dress measures 56 cm (22 in) around the chest and 64 cm (25 in) long

☞ MATERIALS

33 cm × 23 cm (13 in × 9 in) of fine white linen,
   36 threads to 2.5 cm (1 in), for the yoke
Tacking (basting) thread
Tapestry needle size 26
Embroidery hoop (optional)
DMC 6-stranded embroidery floss: see the thread
   list on the right
Dressmaker's graph paper
1.3 m (50 in) of white lawn, 112 cm (44 in) wide
Matching sewing thread
Two white buttons, 6 mm (¼ in) across
1.7 m (1¾ yds) of pink ribbon, 12 mm (½ in) wide

☞ THREAD LIST

577	pale lemon yellow	3354	pink
725	yellow	335	deep pink
783	golden yellow	304	red
921	rust	524	sage green
818	pale pink	3012	olive green

☞ THE EMBROIDERY

Mark the vertical center line of the linen with tacking (basting) stitches and then mark the horizontal positioning line about 8 cm (3 in) in from the bottom edge. Work, as you prefer, in the hand or a hoop (see page 142).

Following the color key and the chart, where one square represents three threads of fabric, work the embroidery outwards from the middle, using two strands of thread in the needle. Leaving the tacking (basting) stitches in place, steam-press the embroidery on the wrong side.

☞ CUTTING OUT THE FABRIC

Enlarge the pattern pieces on page 27 onto dressmaker's graph paper (see page 143). Seam allowances of 1 cm (⅜ in) are included. Transfer all construction marks, then cut out.

Following the cutting layout on page 27, place the pattern pieces on the straight grain of the white lawn and cut out as instructed. Cut the neckband on the bias grain, as indicated in the diagram.

For the front yoke, align the tacking (basting) stitches on the linen with the dashed lines on the pattern before cutting out.

. . . we are hereby made the children of grace.

BOOK OF COMMON PRAYER

☞ MAKING UP THE DRESS

Machine-stitch the skirt, side seams together, using small French seams (see page 146).

On the skirt front, run a double row of gathering stitches between the points marked, and gently pull up the gathers to fit the bottom edge of the front yoke.

Fold the skirt back in half and cut an 18 cm (7 in) opening down the center back. Gather the two top edges, at each side of the opening, and fit them to the two back yoke sections as for the front. With right sides together, pin and machine-stitch the front and back yoke to the skirt. Press the seams upwards.

With right sides together, stitch the shoulder seams and press them open.

To neaten the back opening, pin the facing in place with right sides together and machine-stitch, pivoting the needle at the lower point of the opening before returning along the second side. Make a single turning on the facing, fold it to the wrong side of the opening and hem by hand, carefully stitching into the previously made stitches. Press.

Bind the neck edge with bias strip in the same way, hand-stitching it on the inside.

With right sides together, join the underarm seam on each sleeve and press open. Gather the bottom edge of the sleeve and apply the sleeve band as for the neck, first joining the band into a circle. Gather both sleeve heads and, with right sides together, pin them into the armholes, matching the sleeve seams to the side seams.

To close the dress, make two vertical buttonholes, 8 mm (⅜ in) long: one placed just below the neck binding and the second just above the yoke seam (see page 148 for making buttonholes). Sew on the buttons to correspond.

For the hem, make a single 1 cm (⅜ in) fold and then a 6 cm (2¼ in) fold. Pin and slipstitch in place. Lightly press. Using a single strand each of pink 3354 and yellow 725, work two rows of running stitches around the hem and neck edge to finish

Stitch ribbon around the dress just above the yoke/skirt seam, using tiny slipstitches along both sides. Cut an 8 cm (3 in) length and make a tiny bow, folding in the ends and wrapping another small piece over them; stitch at the back. Cut the remaining ribbon in half and attach long tails to the center front; cover the ends with the bow and then stitch through all layers to secure.

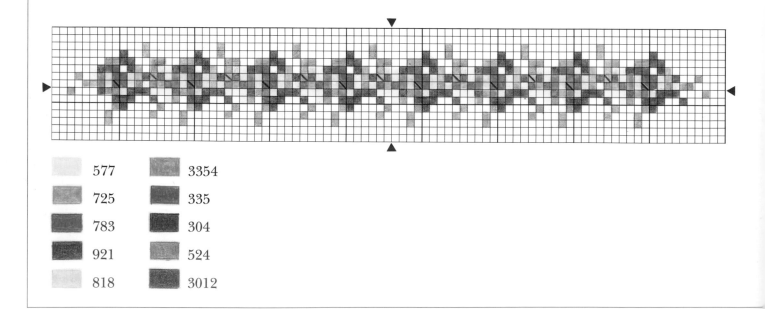

▢ 577	▦ 3354		
▦ 725	▦ 335		
▦ 783	▦ 304		
▦ 921	▦ 524		
▢ 818	▦ 3012		

112 cm (44 in) wide

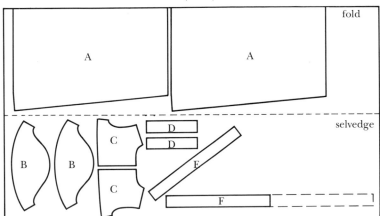

Cutting layout

A – skirt
B – sleeve
C – back bodice
D – sleeve band
E – neckbinding
F – back opening facing

Each square = 2.5 cm (1 in)

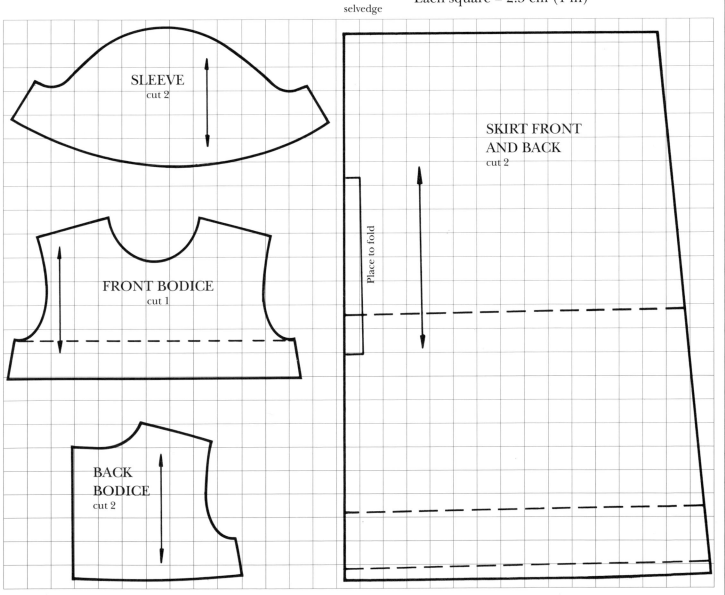

BABY'S BONNET

*In the past, new babies were often greeted with gifts bearing
beautiful inscriptions such as 'Welcome little stranger' and 'Welcome sweet
love' and these were the inspiration for this old-fashioned christening
(or sun) bonnet. Based on a traditional style, the bonnet is gathered into a
central crown and the cross-stitched band, complete with the
baby's name and a motto, is applied on top.*

The bonnet measures 37 cm (14½ in) around the
front edge

☞ MATERIALS

40 cm (16 in) of 5 cm (2 in) wide, white Aida
   band, 15 threads to 2.5 cm (1 in)
Tacking (basting) thread
Tapestry needle size 24
DMC 6-strand embroidery floss: see the thread list
   on the right
Dressmaker's graph paper
56 cm × 20 cm (22 in × 8 in) of white cotton
   broderie anglaise fabric
Matching sewing thread
50 cm (20 in) of white broderie anglaise trim,
   3 cm (1¼ in) wide
40 cm (16 in) of white bias binding,
   12 mm (½ in) wide
1 m (40 in) of white satin ribbon, 15 mm (⅝ in)
   wide, for the ties

☞ THREAD LIST

472	lime green	962	pink
725	yellow	309	deep pink
211	pale mauve	3364	green
963	pale pink	3346	dark green

☞ THE EMBROIDERY

Following the alphabet given on pages 156 and
157, draw in your chosen name in the space
provided on the chart. Should your name be
longer than Lisbeth, omit the center flower motif
and add a comma between the name and 'my
love', adjusting the outer motifs if needed.

Mark the center of the Aida band both ways
with tacking (basting) stitches. Following the color
key and chart, where each square represents one
stitch, embroider the design, working outwards
from the middle, using two strands of thread in
the needle. Remove the tacking (basting) stitches
and steam-press the finished embroidery on the
wrong side.

▨	3364	▨	309
▨	3346	▨	725
▨	963	▨	211
▨	962	▨	472

Repeat center motif

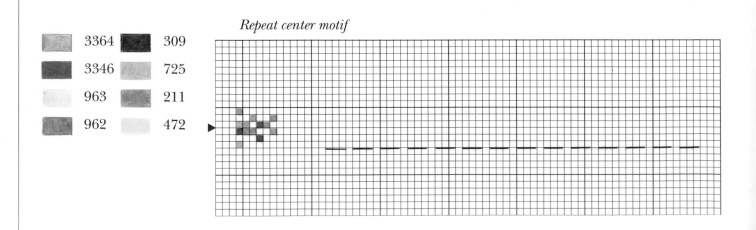

Repeat center motif

*M*ercy and truth are met together
Righteousness and peace have kissed each other
Truth shall flourish out of the earth: and
righteousness hath looked down from heaven.

THE PRAYER BOOK, 1662

MAKING UP THE BONNET

Enlarge the bonnet pattern pieces below
onto dressmaker's graph paper (see page 143),
then cut them out from the broderie anglaise
fabric. Seam allowances of 12 mm (½ in) are
included.

With the right sides together, tack (baste) and
machine stitch the center back seam of the main
section. Run a double row of gathering threads
around the back of the bonnet as indicated on the
pattern. Pull up the gathers evenly and, with the
right sides together, stitch the bonnet section to
the crown. Trim the seam to 6 mm (¼ in), snip
into the curved seam allowance and finger-press
to the inside. Similarly, make a hem on the
broderie anglaise lining, pin and hem in place to
neaten the crown.

FINISHING THE BONNET

Finish the front edge with broderie anglaise trim,
stitching with the wrong sides together. This seam
will be covered by the embroidered band.

Pin and tack (baste) the band in place,
matching the raw edges of the band to the neck
edge. Using two strands of green 472, hand-stitch
the band with one row of running stitch on each
long side.

Bind the neck edge with bias binding (see page
147), turning in the short edges to neaten.
Before hemming the binding on the
wrong side, cut the ribbon in half,
pleat one end of each tie and
slip them inside the bias binding
at each front edge, as shown on
the pattern piece.

Each square = 2.5 cm (1 in)

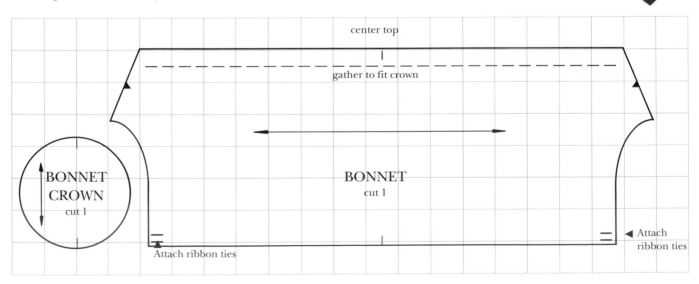

center top

gather to fit crown

BONNET
CROWN
cut 1

BONNET
cut 1

Attach ribbon ties

Attach
ribbon ties

BABY'S FIRST SLIPPERS

When I came to design these baby's first slippers, I was reminded of those I made in cream satin for my own granddaughter's christening. At the time, she was ten months old and, although she could walk reasonably well, we felt she should be carried so I decided to embroider the soles as well as the tops of her slippers. After all it is the feet, more often than not, that a baby in arms shows off rather splendidly. These little slippers are made from fine white evenweave fabric, embroidered with the baby's initials on top and a cluster of rosebuds on the soles.

The slippers are one size, measuring 10 cm (4 in) along the length of the sole

☞ MATERIALS
30 cm (12 in) square of fine white evenweave fabric, 32 threads to 2.5 cm (1 in)
Tacking (basting) thread in a dark color
Embroidery hoop (optional)
DMC 6-strand embroidery floss: see the thread list below
Tapestry needle size 26
Tracing paper and pencil
46 cm (18 in) square of white spotted voile for the lining
1 m (40 in) of white satin ribbon, 6 mm (¼ in) wide, for the ties
Matching sewing thread
Two pearl buttons, 6 mm (¼ in) across

☞ THREAD LIST

927	pale grey green	326	deep pink
819	very pale pink	471	medium green
761	pale pink	3051	deep green
899	medium pink		

☞ THE EMBROIDERY
You will find it easier to work the embroidery before cutting out the fabric. Select your chosen initials from the alphabet on pages 152 and 153. Following the positioning diagram on the right, fold the evenweave fabric vertically in half. Using tacking (basting) stitches, mark the vertical central line and the horizontal positioning lines shown in blue on the diagram, then the center lines on the slipper shapes marked in red.

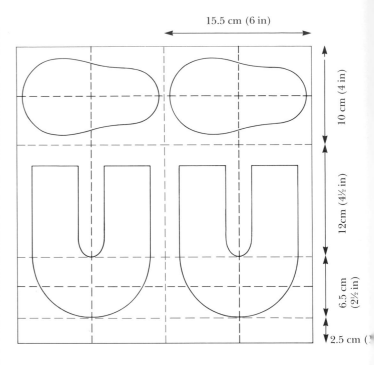

This positioning diagram shows how to work out the position of the embroidery on the fabric before the slipper shapes are cut out.

With your fabric stretched in a hoop, if preferred (see page 142), and two strands of thread in the needle, begin the embroidery working one cross stitch over two threads of fabric. Follow the chart, where each square represents one stitch (ie two threads), making sure you match the center of the chart with the red center of your tacking (basting) stitches, then work outwards from the middle to complete the embroidery. Do not remove the tacking (basting) stitches: these are needed when you cut out the slippers.

When the first baby laughed for the first time,
the laugh broke into a thousand pieces and
they all went skipping about, and that was
the beginning of fairies.

Peter Pan,
J M BARRIE

CUTTING OUT THE SLIPPERS

Make paper templates for the sole and the slipper top by tracing around the patterns on page 34 – 8 mm (5⁄16 in) seam allowances are included. Mark the center lines as indicated and cut out the templates. Pin each pattern piece over the embroidery, carefully matching the red center lines, then cut out the fabric. Repeat for the second sole and slipper top. Remove all the tacking (basting) stitches.

MAKING THE LINING

Fold the voile diagonally in half, crease the foldline and cut across. From one long edge, cut a 2.5 cm (1 in) wide bias strip for binding the slipper tops. From the remaining voile, cut two soles and two slipper tops on the straight grain.

MAKING UP THE SLIPPERS

With the right sides together, machine stitch the center back seam of each slipper top, then press the seam open. Matching the centers, pin each sole to the corresponding top and machine-stitch around. Trim the seam to 6 mm (¼ in), snip into the curved seam allowance and turn to the right side. Finger-press the seam flat. Repeat for the lining but do not turn to the right side.

With the wrong sides together and the centers matching, place the lining inside the slipper, and tack (baste) around the top edge. Bind the top edge using the bias voile strip. Beginning at the center back seam, pin it to the right side, allow an extra 6 mm (¼ in) for the diagonal seam and cut to size. Join the bias strip, (see page 147) and hand stitch the binding in place, using small running stitches. Fold the binding to the wrong

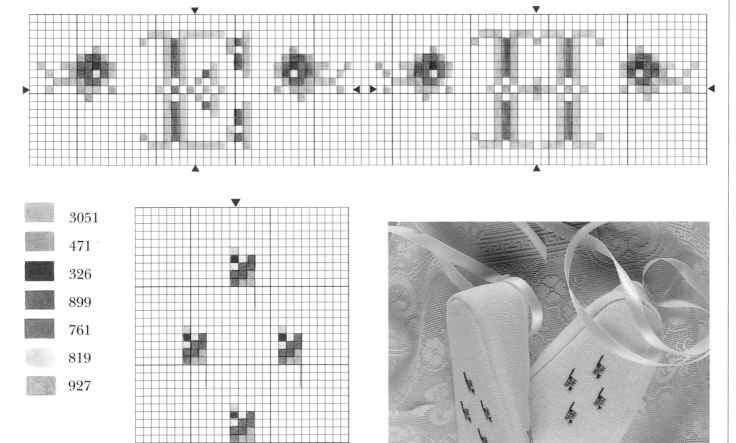

3051
471
326
899
761
819
927

side, turn under a 1 cm (⅜ in) hem and slipstitch
to the wrong side.

Attach the ribbon ties. Cut the ribbon in half
and stitch the center of each tie to the center back
of the slipper, neatly overcasting the edges of the
ribbon and binding on the wrong side. Sew a
button in the center of each tie.

*Cut out one of each of these templates. They include an
8 mm (⁵⁄₁₆ in) seam allowance. Mark the center lines
indicated in red.*

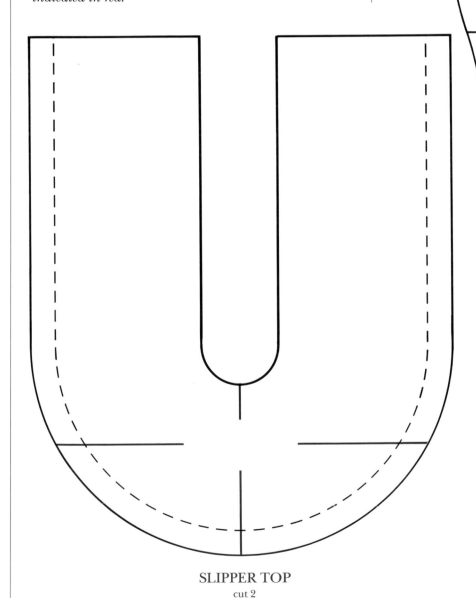

SLIPPER SOLE
cut 2

SLIPPER TOP
cut 2

Weddings and Anniversaries

So let our love as endless prove,
And pure as gold forever.

A Ring Presented to Julia,
ROBERT HERRICK

W E D D I N G   *K* N E E L E R

If the bride and groom are expecting to kneel for any length of time during the marriage service, then a pretty kneeler would be most welcome – two would be ideal but if time allows for making one only, we would expect the groom to be gallant. You may like to add the time and day of the wedding in the space below the heart, for a complete memento of the occasion. Although most weddings today take place on Saturday, it wasn't always so. A bride may have been swayed by the predictions in the rhyme: 'Monday for wealth, Tuesday for health, Wednesday is the best day of all, Thursday for crosses, Friday for losses and Saturday no luck at all'. Perhaps we should take notice.

The finished kneeler measures 38 cm (15 in) square, including the lace trim

☞ MATERIALS
30 cm (12 in) square of off-white linen, 32 threads to 2.5 cm (1 in)
Tacking (basting) thread
Tapestry needle size 26
DMC 6-strand embroidery floss: see the thread list on the right
Tracing paper

25 cm (10 in) square of white cotton fabric for the backing
1 m (40 in) of pre-gathered lace trim, 9 cm (3½ in) wide
Matching sewing thread
About 50 pearl beads, 3 mm (⅛ in) across
25 cm (10 in) square cushion pad.

☞ THREAD LIST
3078	pale yellow	472	pale green
726	yellow	471	green
353	pink	828	blue
351	red	926	grey

O perfect Love, all human thought transcending,
Lowly we kneel in prayer before Thy throne,
That this may be the love which knows no ending
Whom Thou for evermore dost join in one.

Hymn,

DOROTHY FRANCES GURNEY

✒ ADD YOUR OWN NAMES

Using a pencil and referring to the alphabet given on page 149, draw your chosen names in the space provided on the chart, spacing them evenly as seen on the kneeler.

✒ THE EMBROIDERY

Mark the center of the linen both ways with the tacking (basting) stitches. Following the color key and chart, where each square represents one stitch worked over two threads of fabric, begin the cross stitching, working outwards from the center along the flowers of the heart, using two strands of thread in the needle. Complete the heart and then, using grey 926, backstitch the motto and the names.

To work the border, first trace the outline of the quarter section, shown below, and cut it out. Lay the embroidery right side up and place the template in one quarter section, matching the straight lines to the tacked (basted) stitches. Follow the curved line with running stitches using two strands of blue 828 thread in the needle, then repeat in the remaining three quarter sections. Work a second line of running stitches inside the blue, using pink 353 thread.

Fill the border with random straight stitches worked in blue and pink, using a single strand of thread. Trim the finished embroidery to the size of the backing fabric, 25 cm (10 in) square

✒ MAKING UP THE KNEELER

Make up the kneeler following the instructions for the Ring Pillow on page 44, omitting the piping. Attach the pearl beads to the outer edge just inside the lace trim, spacing them about 2 cm (¾ in) apart. (See page 144 for sewing on beads.)

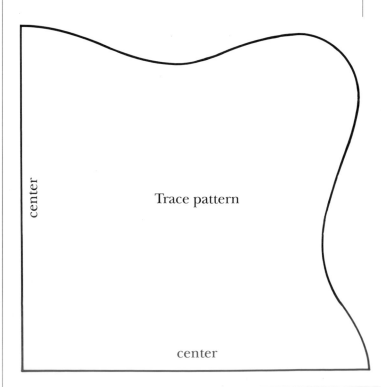

center

Trace pattern

center

One quarter section of the border, actual size. The left-hand vertical line and the bottom horizontal line match the center lines of the embroidery.

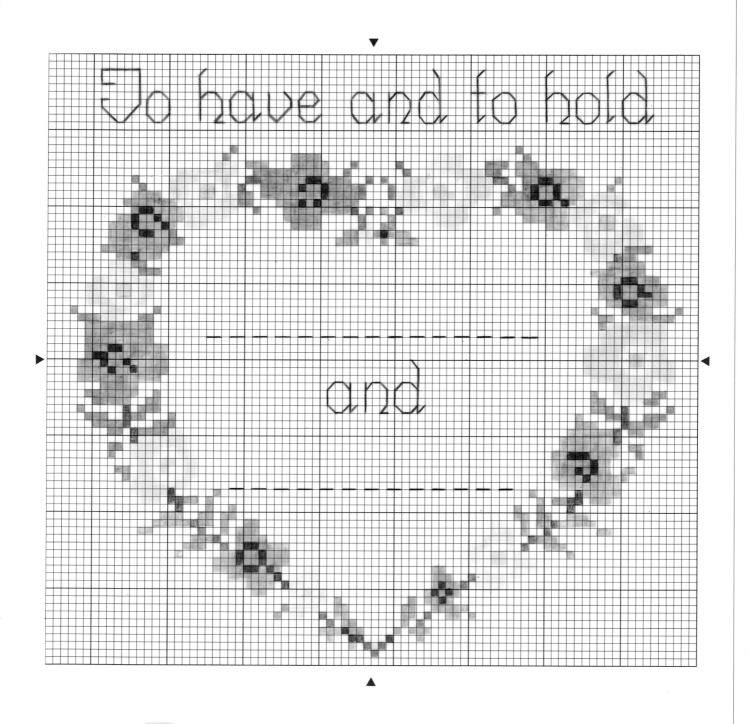

3078   471
726   472
353   828
351   926

$\mathcal{A}$DAM AND $\mathcal{E}$VE PICTURE

*Throughout history, Adam and Eve have been a favorite subject
for embroidery. They are usually seen naked in the Garden of Eden standing on
either side of the apple tree while the serpent twists itself around the tree trunk,
usually with a knowing expression on its face. This has always struck me
as being a particularly poignant moment in time and, somehow, akin
to embarking upon marriage.
Instead of framing the embroidery as a picture, you could make it into a
cushion (for the couple's bed), working it in the color of your choice.*

The finished unframed picture measures
37 cm × 25 cm (14½ in × 10 in)

MATERIALS
48 cm × 38 cm (19 in × 15 in) of off-white linen
   (Zweigart's Cork), 19 threads to 2.5 cm (1 in)
Tacking (basting) thread
Tapestry needle size 24
Embroidery frame (optional)
Three skeins of DMC 6-strand embroidery floss,
   red 349
37 cm × 25 cm (14½ × 10 in) of 3 mm (⅛ in)
   cardboard for mounting the embroidery
37 cm × 25 cm (14½ in × 10 in) of lightweight
   synthetic wadding (batting)
Strong thread or masking tape for securing the
   mounted embroidery
Picture frame of your choice

THE EMBROIDERY
The entire picture is worked in a single color.
Mark the center of the fabric both ways with
tacking (basting) stitches and lightly stretch it in a
frame, if preferred (see page 143).

Following the chart, where each square is equal
to one cross stitch worked over two threads of
fabric, begin in the middle with the tree. Using
three strands of thread in the needle, complete
the tree and the remaining cross stitching.
Outline the tree and serpent using three strands,
as before. Then, using four strands in the needle,
outline the figures of Adam and Eve and the
animals in the foreground. Lightly press the
finished embroidery on the wrong side and retain
the tacking (basting) stitches.

Mount and frame the embroidery following the
instructions on page 148.

*$\mathcal{A}$dam, the goodliest man of men since born
His sons; the fairest of her daughters, Eve.*

Paradise Lost,

JOHN MILTON

349

RING PILLOW

A pretty ring-bearer's pillow will keep the wedding rings tied securely within its ribbon bows until they are required in the marriage service. It will also help to allay the bride and groom's fear that the rings may be misplaced or left behind in the general excitement. Traditionally, it was always believed that the wedding rings were worn on the third finger of the left hand because a vein ran through this finger directly to the heart. Perhaps some of us still think so? After the ceremony the bride can keep the ring pillow as a memento of her wedding day, displaying it, perhaps, on her bed along with other scatter cushions.

With this ring I thee wed, with my body I thee worship.

Solemnization of Matrimony:

BOOK OF COMMON PRAYER

The finished pillow (including the lace trim) measures 25 cm (10 in) square

✐ MATERIALS

23 cm (9 in) square of cream Hardanger, 22 threads to 2.5 cm (1 in)

Tacking (basting) thread

Tapestry needle size 26

Embroidery hoop

20 cm (8 in) square of cream satin for the backing fabric

DMC 6-strand embroidery floss: see the thread list below

DMC 3-strand light gold metallic thread, article 282

90 cm (36 in) of gold and white piping, 3 mm (⅛ in) wide

90 cm (36 in) of white pre-gathered lace trim, 4 cm (1½ in) wide

1.4 m (1½ yds) of pale blue satin ribbon, 6 mm (¼ in) wide

Matching sewing threads

18 cm (7 in) square cushion pad

✐ THREAD LIST

828	pale blue	818	pale pink
472	pale green	224	soft pink
733	olive green	899	sharp pink

Light gold metallic thread

✐ THE EMBROIDERY

From the alphabet given on pages 154 and 155, first select your chosen initials. They will be easier to work from if you can enlarge them on a photocopying machine. Alternatively, draw them on graph paper. Transfer the center lines given on the chart to your printed copy so they will be in the correct position and correspond with the center lines of the fabric.

Mark the center of your fabric both ways with tacking (basting) stitches and then stretch it loosely in a hoop (see page 142). Work the embroidery, beginning with the lettering and using two strands of gold thread in the needle. Following the chart,

work the 'and' first, embroidering one cross stitch over one block of threads. Continue in this way to work your chosen initials.

Using two strands of thread in the needle throughout, and referring to the color key, work the central ring and the pink and blue outlining: one stitch over one block of threads.

Complete the background rosebud pattern and the outer blue line, working each cross stitch over two blocks of threads. Finish by adding the small dots around each bud: one stitch over one block of threads.

Remove the tacking (basting) threads and trim back the edges so that the embroidery measures 20 cm (8 in) square, using the outer pale blue border as a guide.

✐ MAKING UP THE CUSHION

Lay the piping on the right side of the embroidery, placing the raw edge just inside the seam allowance. Tack (baste) and, using the zipper foot on your sewing machine, stitch in place (see page 146). Alternatively, you can hand stitch it. Overlap the two ends neatly, angling the cut edges into the seam allowance. Join together the raw edges of the lace trim with a tiny French seam. With the right sides together, lay the lace on the embroidery, pin and tack (baste) the edge of the lace to the outer edge of the fabric just inside the stitching line for the piping, allowing a little extra fullness around the corners.

Place the backing fabric on top with the right sides together. Tack (baste) and machine stitch around, again using the zipper foot and stitching close to the piping. Leave a 13 cm (5 in) opening in one side. Remove the tacking (basting), trim across the corners and turn the cover through to the right side.

Cut the ribbon into two equal lengths, fold in half and stitch them to the pillow just above the outer blue border, as shown on the chart, using one or two stitches to secure. Insert the cushion pad, turn in the edges of the opening and slipstitch to close.

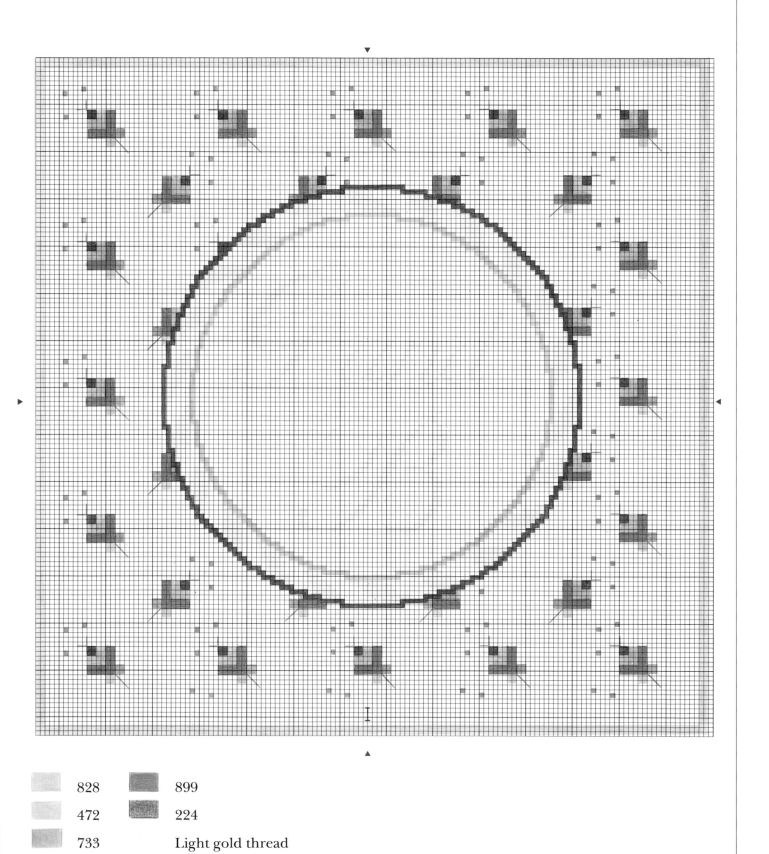

828

899

472

224

733

Light gold thread

818

New Baby

Father asked us what was God's noblest works. Anna said men, *but I said* babies. *Men are often bad; but babies never are.*

Early Diary,
LOUISA MAY ALCOTT

BABY'S PILLOW

*The head of a very small baby is not, of course, laid down to sleep on a pillow but,
as an infant begins to sit up, a pretty pillow such as this can be kept at the foot of the crib
or in the stroller and, when needed, placed behind the baby to offer comfort, support and
security. I have purposely placed the design towards the top part of the pillow so that it
can be seen to full effect.*

The finished pillow measures 33 cm × 41 cm (13 in × 16 in) including the frill

MATERIALS

40 cm × 33 cm (16 in × 13 in) of white Hardanger, 22 threads to 2.5 cm (1 in)

Tacking (basting) thread

Tapestry needle size 26

DMC 6-strand embroidery floss: see the thread list below

33 cm × 25 cm (13 in × 10 in) of white cotton for the backing

2.3 m (2½ yds) of white broderie anglaise trim, 6.5 cm (2½ in) wide

1 m (40 in) of narrow white ribbon, 3 mm (⅛ in) wide

33 cm × 25 cm (13 in × 10 in) cushion pad

10 pearl buttons, preferably old, (optional)

Matching sewing thread

THREAD LIST

772	light green	601	deep pink
726	yellow	471	green
783	golden yellow	800	pale blue
776	pale pink	799	blue
956	pink		

THE EMBROIDERY

Mark the center of the evenweave fabric both ways with tacking (basting) stitches and begin the cross stitch embroidery, working outwards from the middle. Using two strands of thread in the needle and following the color key and chart, where one square represents two threads of fabric, work the ribbon first. Add the flowers and then finish with the backstitching and motto.

To work the border, attach the narrow ribbon in the position marked on the chart, securing it with cross stitches embroidered in random blocks of colors. Overlap the ends and stitch to secure them under a block of cross stitches.

Using a single strand each of the palest colors (772, 726, 776 and 800), work small straight stitches at random to make an inner border (the stitches on the chart are shown as a guide). Remove the tacking (basting) stitches and steampress the finished embroidery on the wrong side. Trim the embroidery to the size of the backing fabric, 33 cm × 25 cm (13 in × 10 in).

Make up the pillow following the instructions for the Ring Pillow on page 44, omitting the piping. Attach the pearl buttons to the outer edge, if wished, following the diagram on the right.

*S*ilently one by one,
In the infinite meadows of heaven
Blossomed the lovely stars,
The forget-me-nots of the angels.

Evangeline,

H W LONGFELLOW

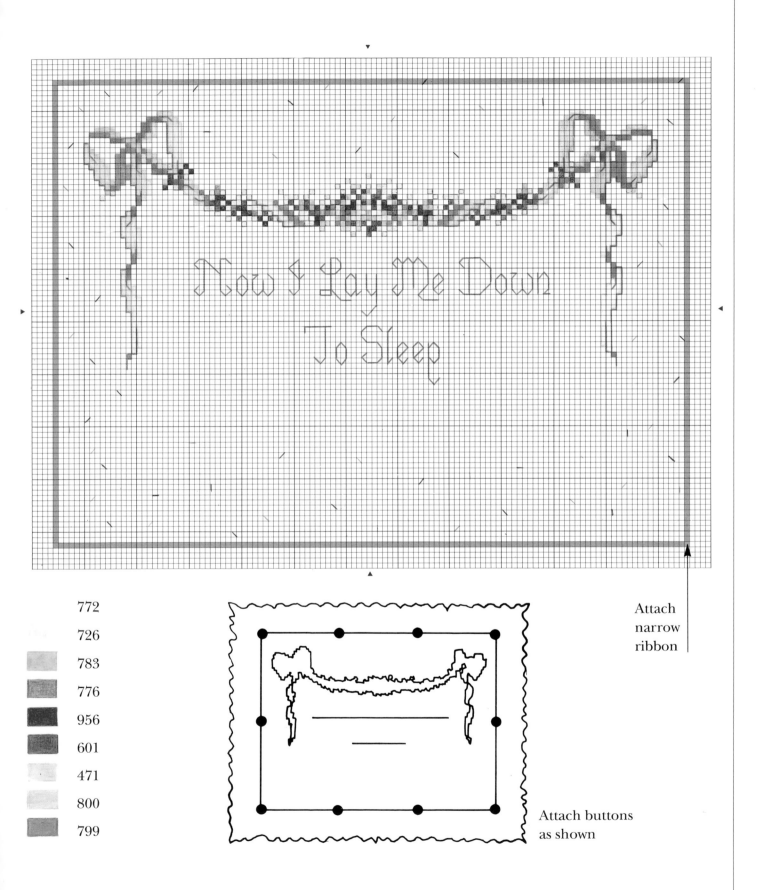

772

726

783

776

956

601

471

800

799

Attach
narrow
ribbon

Attach buttons
as shown

BABY'S CRIB COVER

Welcoming a new baby is always an exciting experience – and what better way to show your love than with beautiful gifts you have made yourself. For this little crib or stroller cover, which is based on a patchwork quilt construction, I have shown decorative hearts in the squares with a different motif in each one to represent good luck, joy, peace and tranquillity, as well as the baby's first names.

Another delightful idea would be to follow the tradition of a friendship quilt and, before the baby arrives, ask friends to work the four motif squares for you, adding the baby's name when it is born.

Go to sleep and good night;
In a rosy twilight
Snuggle deep in your bed.
God will watch, never fear,
While Heaven draws near.

Traditional German Slumber Song,
ADAPTED BY LOUIS UNTERMEYER

The finished cover measures 69 cm × 49 cm (27 in × 19½ in) including the frill

☞ MATERIALS
Metric graph paper
Six 20 cm (8 in) squares of white Hardanger, 16 threads to 2.5 cm (1 in)
Tacking (basting) thread
Tapestry needle size 24
Small embroidery hoop (optional)
DMC 6-strand embroidery floss: see the thread list on page 52
1 m (40 in) of white broderie anglaise, 152 cm (60 in) wide
2.7 m (3 yds) of white, pre-gathered broderie anglaise trim, 5 cm (2 in) wide
66 cm × 47 cm (26 in × 18½ in) medium-weight synthetic wadding (batting)
White sewing thread
12 pearl buttons, 6 mm (¼ in) across (optional)

THREAD LIST

445	pale yellow	472	pale green
307	yellow	907	green
742	orange	913	viridian green
351	red	3042	mauve
761	pink	3752	blue

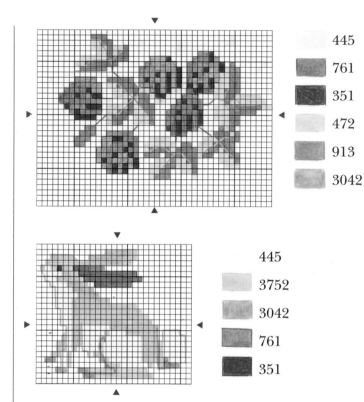

THE EMBROIDERY

Following the alphabet on pages 150 and 151, draw your chosen name on metric graph paper or, alternatively, repeat two of the motifs given.

On each of the white Hardanger squares, which include a 2.5 cm (1 in) allowance all around, mark the center both ways with tacking (basting) stitches and place in a small hoop, if preferred (see page 142).

Following the embroidery diagram, the appropriate color key and chart, where each square equals one cross stitch, complete the embroidery on all six squares, using two strands of thread in the needle throughout.

Note that the butterfly wings are outlined in red 351; the veins of the clover leaves, the dove's wing and the rabbit's tail in mauve 3042; the dove's body in orange 742, the dove's tail and the rabbit's body in blue 3752.

Using the tacking (basting) stitches to measure accurately, trim the edges of the squares, leaving a 12 mm (½ in) seam allowance. Remove tacking (basting) and steam-press on the wrong side.

MAKING UP THE COVER

From the broderie anglaise fabric, cut out the following rectangular pattern pieces: Crib cover back, 64 cm × 44.5 cm (25 in × 17½ in); Crib cover front, cut two side pieces 56 cm × 6.5 cm (22 in × 2½ in) (F and G on the positioning guide on page 54); cut two pieces (top and bottom) 44.5 cm × 6.5 cm (17½ in × 2½ in) (marked H and I); cut two across pieces 37 cm × 6.5 cm (14½ in × 2½ in) (marked D and E); cut three short upright pieces 18 cm × 6.5 cm (7 in × 2½ in) (marked A, B and C). Seam allowances of 12 mm (½ in) are included.

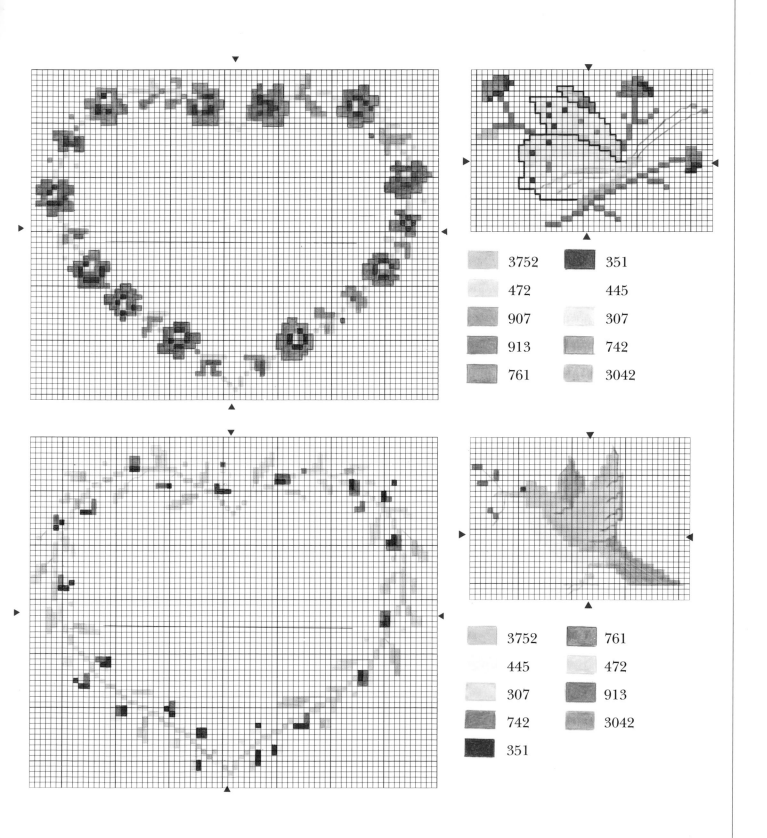

	3752		351
	472		445
	907		307
	913		742
	761		3042

	3752		761
	445		472
	307		913
	742		3042
	351		

Following the positioning guide (right), lay out the embroidered squares in sequence (see right) and then the piecing strips of broderie anglaise. Tack (baste) and machine-stitch the three shorter rows across, beginning by joining together pieces 1, A, and 2, as shown in the diagram. Stitch with the evenweave on top so that you can keep a straight line along the grain. Press the seams open. Join the two across rows D and E in the same way. Then add the side pieces F and G, followed by H and I to finish piecing the top.

☛ THE INTERLINING

Lay the backing fabric wrong side up, place the wadding (batting) on top and tack (baste) across both ways. Join the raw ends of the broderie anglaise trim using a small French seam. Lay the top section right side up, place the trim with the finished edge matching the raw edge of the fabric and tack (baste) to secure, easing extra fullness around the corners. Machine-stitch across one short edge.

Place the backing and top section with the right sides together, than tack (baste) and machine-stitch around the edge of the cover, leaving a 23 cm (9 in) opening in one short side for turning through. Remove the tacking (basting) stitches, trim across the corners, and turn through to the right side. Lightly steam-press, if necessary. Turn under the seam allowance of the opening and slipstitch to close.

☛ SECURING THE KNOTS

Secure the three layers by tying quilting knots (see page 144) as marked on the positioning guide. With doubled thread in the needle, stitch through the layers, finishing with the knots on the wrong side. For added decoration, attach the buttons, as shown.

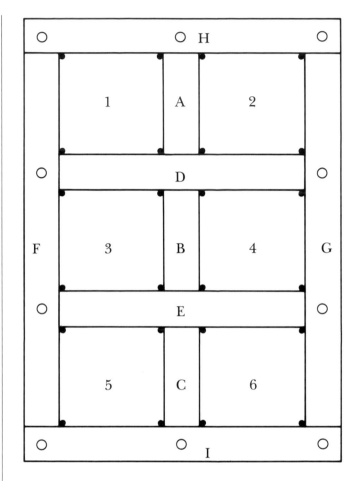

Positioning guide

Place the squares so that the red and yellow hearts are in alternate positions in the three rows.

● Quilting knots
○ Buttons

And still she slept an azure-lidded sleep,
In blanched linen, smooth and lavender'd.

Fairy Song,

JOHN KEATS

BABY'S FIRST JACKET

Baby clothes are always a welcome gift and this little linen and voile-lined jacket, with its delicately embroidered flowers and lace trim, is pretty enough for a christening. Like the christening robe on page 24, the pattern is one I used for my own children's baptism and is based on a traditional Magyar style from Hungary where the sleeves and jacket are cut in one piece. It is also one of the easiest patterns to adjust for larger or smaller sizes.

The best things come in small parcels.

Proverb

The jacket fits a 60 cm (24 in) chest and measures 25 cm (10 in) long.

☞ MATERIALS

Two 72 cm × 36 cm (28 in × 14 in) pieces of white linen, 36 threads to 2.5 cm (1 in)
Tacking (basting) thread
Tapestry needle size 26
Embroidery hoop
DMC 6-strand embroidery floss: see the thread list below
Dressmaker's graph paper
White sewing thread
110 cm (43 in) of pre-gathered cotton lace, 2 cm (¾ in) wide
60 cm (24 in) of contrast ribbon, 1 cm (⅜ in) wide
Two 1 cm (⅜ in) buttons

☞ THREAD LIST

745	pale yellow	794	pale blue
725	yellow	793	blue
722	orange	472	pale green
554	mauve	3347	green

☞ THE EMBROIDERY

Cut one piece of linen widthwise in half to give two jacket front pieces each measuring 36 cm (14 in) square. Referring to the chart, tack (baste) the positioning lines for the embroidery on one of the pieces, placing the vertical line 8 cm (3 in) from the side edge and the horizontal line 8 cm (3 in) up from the bottom edge. Repeat in reverse for the second jacket front. Stretch the fabric in a hoop (see page 142).

Following the color key and the chart, where each square is equal to one stitch worked over three threads of fabric, begin the embroidery, working outwards from the center using two strands of thread in the needle. Complete the cross stitching and then add the backstitch details. Repeat on the second front. Lightly steam-press on the wrong side but keep the tacking (basting) stitches in place.

☞ MAKING UP THE JACKET

Enlarge the pattern pieces (opposite) onto dressmaker's graph paper (see page 143). Seam allowances of 12 mm (½ in) are included. Transfer all construction marks and draw in the positioning lines for the embroidery, before cutting out. Lay the embroidered fronts right side up, pin the pattern on top with the positioning lines matching, then cut out. Remember to cut out the second front in reverse so that the embroidery is at the center front of the jacket. From the second piece of linen, folded widthwise in half, cut out the jacket back placing the center back to the fold. Cut out the lining from the voile in the same way.

With the right sides of the jacket fronts and jacket back together, pin and machine-stitch across the shoulder and sleeve seams. Press the seams open. Join the side and underarm seams in the same way. Repeat for the lining.

Place the jacket and lining right sides together, pin and machine-stitch around the neck, down the front pieces and around the bottom edge in a continuous movement. Trim the seam to 6 mm (¼ in), clip into the curves and across the corners before turning to the right side through one open sleeve. Finger-press the seams flat.

Make 12 mm (½ in) turnings on the sleeve edges and slipstitch to secure, easing the lining inside the outer sleeve edge. Using matching sewing thread, topstitch around the edges of the jacket with small running stitches.

Trim the neck and sleeve edges with lace, hem-stitching it in place and overlapping the raw edges to neaten.

Cut the ribbon into two halves and attach to the front edges of the neck, sliding it under the loose edge of the lace trim and catching it with a single stitch. Sew the buttons on top, stitching through all layers. Using four strands of thread, work yellow and blue French knots around the neck and sleeves, placing them about 12 mm (½ in) apart.

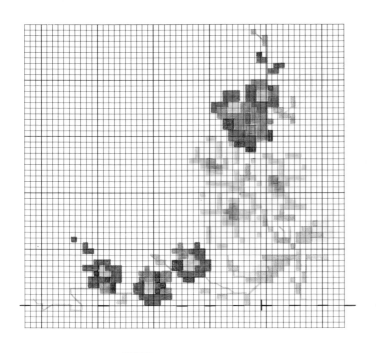

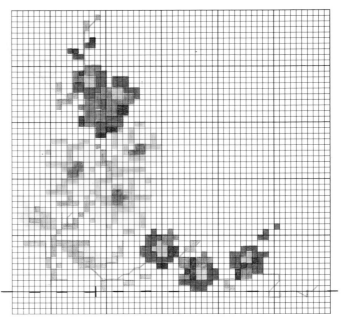

745

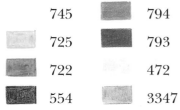725

722

554

794

793

472

3347

Each square = 2.5 cm (1 in)

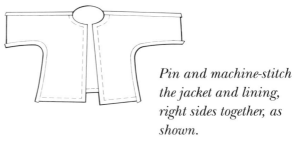

*Pin and machine-stitch
the jacket and lining,
right sides together, as
shown.*

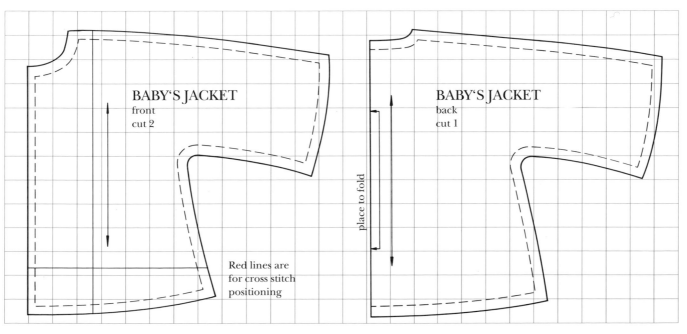

BABY'S JACKET
front
cut 2

BABY'S JACKET
back
cut 1

place to fold

Red lines are
for cross stitch
positioning

Confirmation

*Be strong and of good courage;
be not afraid, neither be thou dismayed;
for the Lord thy God is with thee
whithersoever thou goest.*

Joshua Chapter 1, Verse 9

BABY IN THE BULLRUSHES

This has always been one of my favourite bible stories epitomizing the love a mother has for her child. In the story, Moses was born in Egypt at a time when the Hebrews were slaves, and one of the kings had ordered that all new-born Hebrew boys were to be killed. His mother, Jochabed, desparate to save her baby, put Moses in a reed basket among the rushes on the bank of the river Nile, hoping someone would take pity on him. The king's daughter came to bathe in the river and found the baby. The princess sent for a Hebrew woman to look after the baby, and the woman she chose was Jochabed.

This simple act of faith and courage is very touching and, because it shows that even the most desperate of situations can be overcome, I thought it would make an appropriate subject and gift for a daughter or young girl at her confirmation.

The finished unframed picture measures
22 cm × 18 cm (8½ in × 7 in)

☞ MATERIALS
30 cm × 28 cm (12 in × 11 in) of blue Aida fabric,
   14 threads to 2.5 cm (1 in)
Tacking (basting) thread
Tapestry needle size 24
Embroidery frame (optional)

DMC 6-strand embroidery floss, see the thread list
   overleaf
22 cm × 18 cm (8½ in × 7 in) of 3 mm (⅛ in)
   cardboard for mounting the embroidery
22 cm × 18 cm (8½ in × 7 in) of lightweight
   synthetic wadding (batting)
Masking tape or strong thread
Picture frame of your choice

THREAD LIST

948	flesh	341	pale mauve
3341	deep apricot	340	mauve
3354	pink	611	brown
602	deep pink	472	lime green
335	red (two skeins)	733	light olive green
445	lemon yellow	936	deep olive green
444	yellow	413	grey
3364	soft green	702	grass green
334	blue	320	green
797	deep blue	561	dark green

THE EMBROIDERY

Mark the center of your fabric both ways with tacking (basting) stitches and stretch it in a frame, if preferred (see page 143). Following the color key and the chart, where each square represents one stitch, begin the embroidery working outwards from the center. Complete the design using two strands of thread in the needle throughout.

When stitching the bullrushes behind Jochabed, work the darker stems and leaves first and then fill in the remaining areas with the two lighter greens, as shown on the chart. Finish the cross stitching and then outline the baby's pillow and around the lower part of the duck with red 335, using backstitch. Similarly, outline the duck's head and neck with blue 797.

Mount and frame the completed picture following the instructions on page 148.

So she got a rush basket for him, made it watertight with clay and tar, laid him in it and put it among the reeds by the bank of the Nile.

Exodus II Verse 3,

NEW ENGLISH BIBLE

948
3341
3354
335
445
444
3364
334
341
340
611
472
733
936
797
413
702
320
561
602

BIBLE
BOOKMARK

*Calling on a friend recently I noticed that her family bible lay open on her table
with a pretty bookmark to keep the page. I came away thinking she was the kind
of mother who, perhaps, after family prayers or similar discussion, would have
left the relevant page marked for her children to read in their own time.
This gave me the idea that a bible bookmark would make a wonderful gift
for a young person at their confirmation. Alternatively, you may belong to a
church or prayer group where a bible bookmark would be a practical and
acceptable gift.*

*God is love; and he that dwelleth in love dwelleth in
God, and God in him.*

John I Chapter 4, Verse 16

The finished bible bookmark measures
34.5 cm × 9 cm (13½ in × 3½ in) including the
ribbon underneath

☞ MATERIALS

One 22 cm × 9 cm (8½ in × 3½ in) white prepared
   lace-edged bookmark, 18 threads to 2.5 cm (1 in)
Tacking (basting) thread
Tapestry needle size 26
DMC 6-strand embroidery floss: see the thread list
   below
66 cm (26 in) of cream and gold damask ribbon,
   6.5 cm (2½ in) wide
Matching sewing thread

☞ THREAD LIST

Light gold metallic thread	817 red
911 green	796 blue

☞ THE EMBROIDERY

Mark the center of the bookmark both ways with
tacking (basting) stitches and, working from
the chart, where one square equals one cross
stitch, begin the embroidery in the middle. Follow
the color key and use two strands of thread in the
needle for both the gold and colored threads.

Complete the cross stitching and then outline
the cross and jewels in backstitch. Similarly, work
the ray lines in backstitch. Remove the tacking
(basting) stitches and steam-press on the wrong
side, if necessary.

☞ MAKING UP THE BOOKMARK

Cut tails into the raw edges of the ribbon to a
depth of 5 cm (2 in). Fold the ribbon so that the
tails are about 12 mm (½ in) apart. Place the
bookmark on top, about 4 cm (1½ in) from the
folded edge then, using gold thread, attach it to
the top ribbon only with cross stitches as shown on
the chart in yellow.

Using matching thread, secure both ribbons
with two or three small stitches placed in the lace
edging of the bookmark.

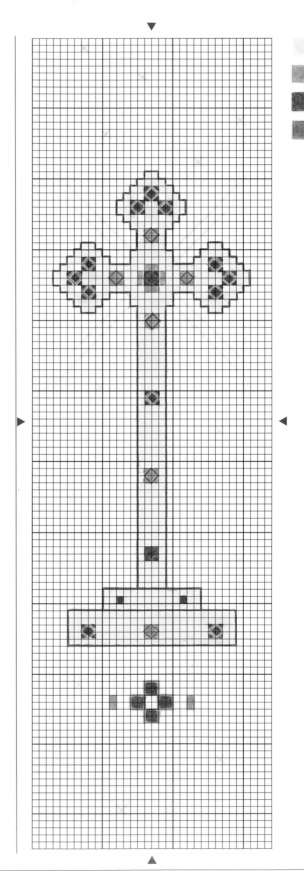

LIGHT
GOLD
THREAD

911

817

796

Favorite Pets

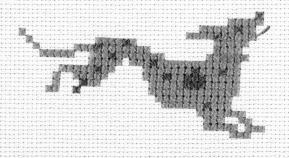

Animals are such agreeable friends –
they ask no questions, they pass no criticism.

Scenes of Clerical Life,
GEORGE ELIOT

CAT PORTRAIT

A cherished pet becomes an important part of the household and is, naturally, often photographed, drawn and painted and hung along with portraits of the family. Cats, in particular, make excellent subjects for artistic expression: the colors and patterns of their coats and their individual characters lend themselves well to all kinds of media, including cross stitch – as seen in this portrait of Boris, a Burmilla with great beauty and charm.

The finished unframed picture measures
19 cm × 14 cm (7½ in × 5½ in)

☞ MATERIALS

29.5 cm × 23 cm (11½ in × 9 in) of light grey Aida fabric, 14 threads to 2.5 cm (1 in)

Tacking (basting) thread

Tapestry needle size 24

Embroidery hoop (optional)

DMC 6-strand embroidery floss: see the thread list on page 68

19 cm × 14 cm (7½ in × 5½ in) of 3 mm (⅛ in) cardboard for mounting the embroidery

19 cm × 14 cm (7½ in × 5½ in) of lightweight synthetic wadding (batting)

Strong thread or masking tape for securing the mounted embroidery

Picture frame of your choice

☞ THREAD LIST

950	flesh	3779	pink
822	cream	351	red
676	pale yellow	834	yellow
3032	fawn	3348	green
869	brown	3766	blue
647	grey	3012	olive green
310	black		

☞ THE EMBROIDERY

Mark the center of your fabric both ways with
tacking (basting) stitches and stretch it in a hoop,
if preferred (see page 142). Following the color
key and the chart, where one square represents
one stitch, begin the embroidery using two strands
of thread in the needle throughout. Work
outwards from the center, completing all the cross
stitching of the cat, then embroider the pattern
on the rug before filling in the background.
Finish by adding the backstitch details and the
whiskers in stem stitch (see the diagram below).

Mount and frame the completed picture
following the instructions on page 148.

☞ STEM
STITCH WHISKERS

For a single line, such
as the whiskers, work
from left to right along
the stitch line. Keeping
the thread to the left
of the needle, make
small, even stitches.

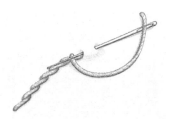

☞ CAPTURING A LIKENESS

To capture a likeness of your own pet cat, you may
like to chart your own design from a favorite
photograph. If necessary, use a photocopier to
enlarge the photograph to the size of the chart
given here. Rule the outer measurement of the
chart on to a sheet of metric graph paper and
place it on top of the cat print. To make enlarging
easier if you don't have a photocopier, during
daytime hours, attach the two pieces of paper to a
window, aligning the lines. Using a pencil, lightly
trace around the shape of the cat and the main
details. Remove from the window and carefully re-
draw the outlines following the square grid lines.
Referring to your color photograph, or to the
actual pet, color in your drawing with pencil
crayons or paints to complete your working chart.
Finally, select matching embroidery threads.

*B efore a Cat will condescend
To treat you as a trusted friend,
Some little token of esteem
Is needed, like a dish of cream.*

Old Possum's Book of Practical Cats,

T S ELIOT

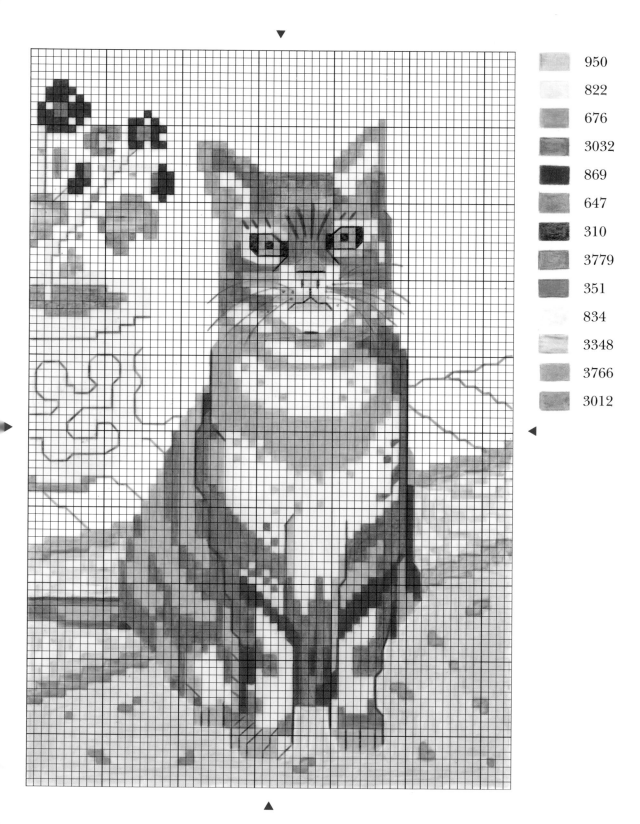

950
822
676
3032
869
647
310
3779
351
834
3348
3766
3012

BIRD PORTRAIT

Pet birds make wonderful subjects for embroidery – their appealing shapes and expressions are fairly easy to capture and those with colorful plumage, like my rainbow lorikeet shown here, sparkle like jewels. Lots of other birds such as parrots, macaws, lovebirds, budgerigars and the best known of all caged birds, the yellow canary, make delightful portraits.

If you don't own one of these birds, and would like to cross stitch a collection of bird portraits, you could make a chart from a photograph or a book illustration following the instructions given on page 68.

The finished unframed picture measures 22 cm × 13.5 cm (8½ in × 5¼ in)

☞ MATERIALS

32 cm × 23 cm (12½ in × 9 in) of yellow Aida fabric, 14 threads to 2.5 cm (1 in)
Tacking (basting) thread
Tapestry needle size 24
DMC 6-strand embroidery floss: see the thread list on the right
22 cm × 13.5 cm (8½ × 5¼ in) of 3 mm (⅛ in) cardboard for mounting the embroidery
22 cm × 13.5 cm (8½ in × 5¼ in) of lightweight synthetic wadding (batting)
Masking tape or strong thread for securing the mounted embroidery.
Picture frame of your choice

☞ THREAD LIST

772	pale avocado		
307	yellow		
725	deep yellow		
3354	pink		
833	golden yellow		
793	blue		
792	royal blue		
350	red	928	light grey
907	lime green	318	grey
701	green	927	pale green grey
732	olive green	3799	dark grey

☞ THE EMBROIDERY

Mark the center of your fabric both ways with tacking (basting) stitches. Following the color key and the chart, where each square is equal to one stitch worked over one intersection of fabric, begin the embroidery in the middle, using two strands of thread in the needle. Work the bird's claws first and then the perch: this will be a good reference point for working the rest of the design. Complete the cross stitching and then work the backstitching on top, using black for the eye, royal blue on the breast and olive green on the bird's wing.

To suggest the grit in the bottom of the cage, make small straight stitches at random, as shown on the chart, using different colored threads.

Mount and frame the completed picture following the instructions on page 148.

Sweet bird, that shunn'st the noise of folly,
Most musical, most melancholy!

JOHN MILTON

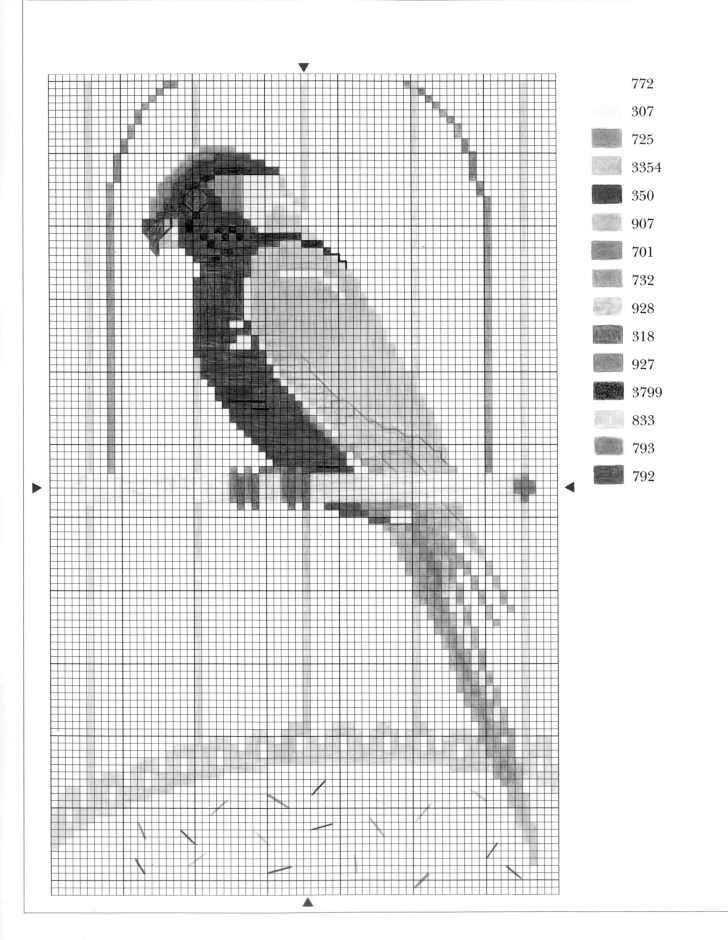

772
307
725
3354
350
907
701
732
928
318
927
3799
833
793
792

DOG TOWEL

What could be a more appealing gift to a devoted dog owner than a towel embroidered with a portrait of their beloved pet. You can choose the most apt dog motif from the selection of alternatives given on page 75 and change the colors to those of your choice. The embroidery is worked on separate bands of evenweave fabric which are then bound around the edges with a contrast color and applied to a purchased hand towel.

The finished dog towel measures 1 m × 50 cm
(40 in × 20 in)

⌐ MATERIALS

Two pieces 59 cm × 10 cm (23 in × 4 in) of cream
   Aida fabric, 14 threads to 2.5 cm (1 in)
Tacking (basting) thread
Tapestry needle size 24
DMC 6-strand embroidery floss: see the thread list
   below
2.5 m (2¾ yds) of turquoise bias binding,
   2.5 cm (1 in) wide
Matching sewing thread
Buff colored hand towel, 1 m × 50 cm
   (40 in × 20 in)

⌐ THREAD LIST

| 648 | light grey | 597 | turquoise blue |
| 414 | grey | 3705 | red |

⌐ THE EMBROIDERY

Mark the center both ways on each band of
evenweave with tacking (basting) stitches. Then,
following the color key and chart, where each
square represents one cross stitch, begin the
embroidery, working outwards from the center,
using two strands of thread in the needle.
Complete both bands. Remove the tacking
(basting) stitches and steam-press on the wrong
side. Trim the edges of the evenweave to measure
53.5 cm × 7 cm (21 in × 2¾ in). Apply bias binding
to the long edges of each band, machine-stitching
it first to the wrong side (see page 147). Fold the
binding to the front and tack (baste) in place.
Make 12 mm (½ in) single folds on each short
side, press and pin the bands in place over the
existing woven bands on the right side of the
towel, then machine-stitch across. Pin a piece of
tissue paper to the wrong side of the towel to
prevent the loops of the pile from getting caught
in the feed below the needle. Similarly, stitch the
short sides using matching thread.

648
414
597
3705
+
quilting
knot

⌒ ATTACHING THE BAND TO THE TOWEL
Using a single strand of red embroidery thread,
secure the evenweave to the towel with quilting
knots (see page 144), stitching through the five
hearts and in positions marked with a cross
through the lettered band, as shown on the chart.

*Alternative
dog motifs*

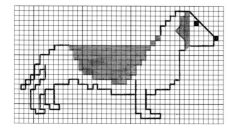

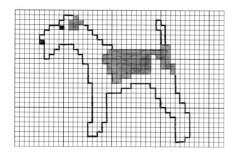

*The dog is man's best friend.
He has a tail on one end.
Up in front he has teeth
And four legs underneath.*

OGDEN NASH

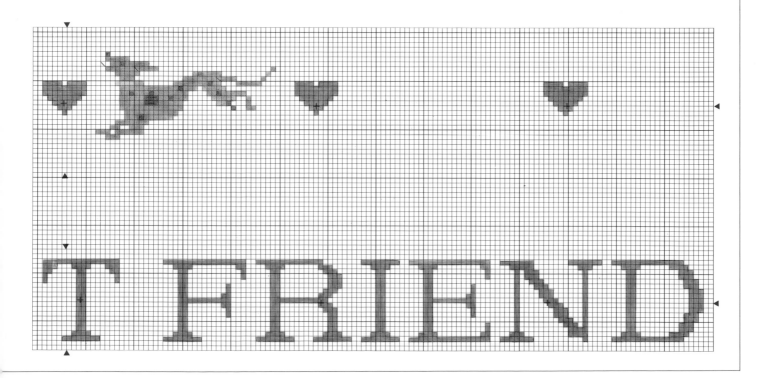

CHAPTER

2

—

NEW

HOME

The House

M id pleasures and palaces though we
may roam,
Be it ever so humble, there's no place
like home.

Clari, the Maid of Milan,
H PAYNE

$\mathcal{H}$OUSE $\mathcal{S}$AMPLER

I feel fortunate to have been brought up in the country with a garden and family pets, and to have been surrounded by beautiful trees, fields and flowers. This was my inspiration for the sampler design which is based on simple traditional lines. An alphabet and numerals are given within the 'garden path' so that you can easily substitute your own name and date or even substitute other motifs to further personalize your sampler.

The finished unframed sampler measures
20 cm × 25 cm (8 in × 10 in)

☞ MATERIALS

36 cm × 31 cm (14 in × 12 in) of natural linen,
  28 threads to 2.5 cm (1 in)
Tacking (basting) thread
Tapestry needle size 26
Embroidery frame
DMC 6-strand embroidery floss: see the thread list
  on the right
25 cm × 20 cm (10 in × 8 in) of 3 mm (⅛ in)
  cardboard for mounting the embroidery
25 cm × 20 cm (10 in × 8 in) of lightweight
  synthetic wadding (batting)

Strong thread or masking tape for securing the
  mounted fabric
Picture frame of your choice

☞ THREAD LIST

726	yellow	733	olive green
783	deep yellow	3761	blue
3354	pink	503	grey green
350	red	958	mid viridian
472	lime green		green
989	mid green	3046	pale gold
991	deep viridian	3032	light brown
	green	610	brown

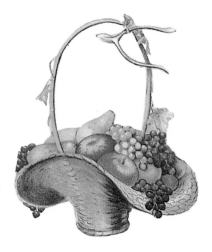

☞ ADDING YOUR OWN NAME

Using the alphabet given with the chart, draw your chosen name and date on a piece of graph paper, matching the grid to that given in the book. If you have a long surname, then use only initials for your first name(s).

☞ THE EMBROIDERY

Mark the center of your fabric both ways with tacking (basting) stitches and stretch it in a frame (see page 143). Following the color key and the chart, where one square equals two threads of fabric, and using two strands of thread in the needle throughout, begin the cross stitching in the middle. Complete the embroidery, working the cross stitching first and then the backstitching. With fine openweave fabrics, it is important not to carry the embroidery threads across the back of the work, otherwise they will show on the right side.

To continue from one stitched area to another, either run the needle under previously made stitches or, on short runs, take the needle vertically or horizontally across the back. Alternatively, knot the thread and begin again underneath an embroidered part.

Work the eyes of the tortoise and the bird with small French knots (see page 145). Carefully trim all the loose ends.

Remove the completed embroidery from the frame but leave the tacking (basting) stitches in place: they will be helpful in centering your fabric on the cardboard.

Mount and frame the completed embroidery following the instructions on page 148.

But what on earth is half so dear –
So longed for – as the hearth of home?

A Little While,

EMILY BRONTE

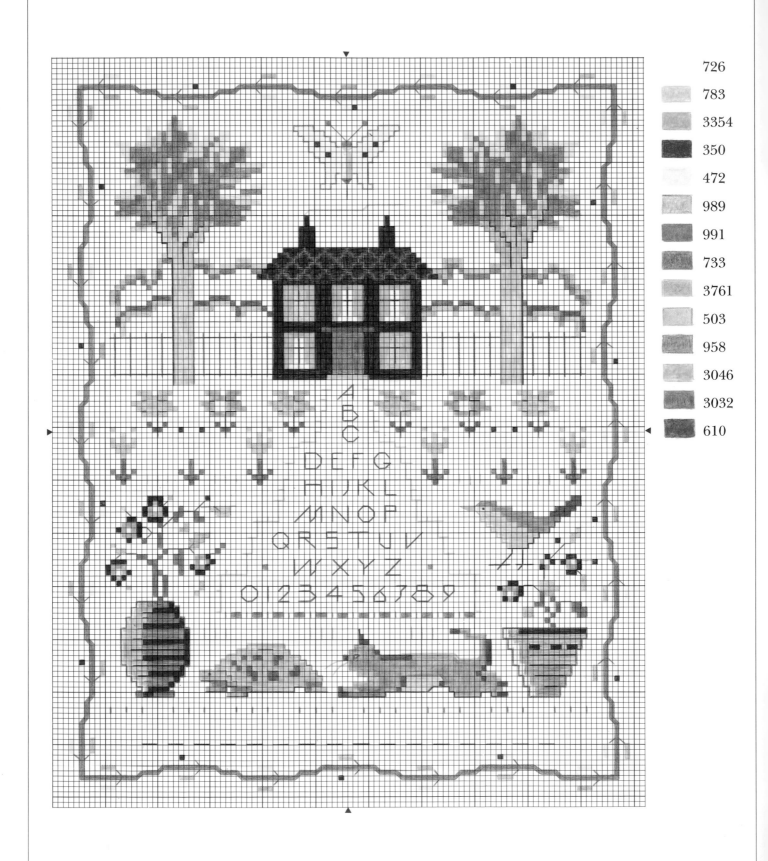

726
783
3354
350
472
989
991
733
3761
503
958
3046
3032
610

Around the Home

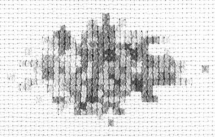

Seek home for rest,
For home is best.

Five Hundred Points of Good Husbandry,

THOMAS TUSSER

Guest Towels

My passion for collecting pretty hand towels started long ago when I was given an Edwardian pair that had belonged to a great aunt. I still have them: they are made from huckaback fabric and, like many other all-white towels of the period, have bands of flowers picked out in a damask weave, and are trimmed with the most delicate hand-crocheted lace.

These were the beginning of my collection which now extends to many other types, including old Turkish towels whose floral decorations are beautifully stitched (on a wide band of evenweave set between pile surfaces) in silk and metallic threads. One or two prettily stitched guest towels, such as these, would make both a decorative and practical gift for friends and relatives moving into a new home or, indeed, a delightful addition for your own bathroom.

You are very welcome to our house:
It must appear in other ways than words.

The Merchant of Venice,

Act V, scene 1

SHAKESPEARE

Each finished towel measures 46 cm × 27 cm (18 in × 10½ in)

☞ MATERIALS

Two purchased guest towels with an integral band of 14 count evenweave fabric, 6 cm (2¼ in) deep
Tacking (basting) thread
Tapestry needle size 24
DMC 6-strand embroidery floss: see the thread lists below

☞ THREAD LISTS

Geometric border

744	pale yellow		3761	blue
3341	deep apricot		524	sage green
972	yellow		733	olive green
3776	tan			

Posy border

3078	pale yellow		3350	magenta
743	yellow		3609	sugar pink
783	deep yellow		340	mauve
721	orange		504	pale green
761	pale pink		502	green
899	pink			

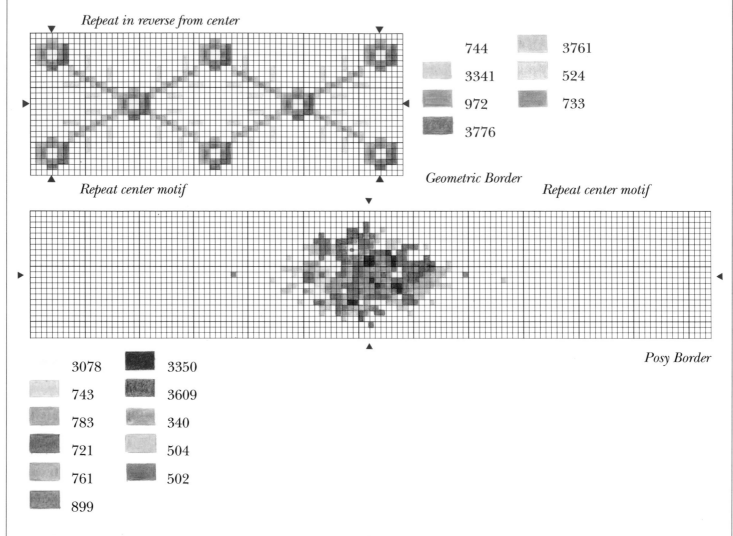

Repeat in reverse from center

744	3761
3341	524
972	733
3776	

Geometric Border

Repeat center motif   *Repeat center motif*

Posy Border

3078	3350
743	3609
783	340
721	504
761	502
899	

☞ THE EMBROIDERY

Both towels are embroidered in the same way. Mark the center of the evenweave band both ways with tacking (basting) stitches . Following the color key and your chosen chart, where each square represents one stitch worked over one intersection of fabric, begin the embroidery working outwards from the center. Use two strands of thread in the needle throughout.

For the geometric border design, complete the first half of the border as shown, then repeat it on the opposite side to complete the design.

For the posy border design, complete the central posy, adding a single French knot in orange 721, as shown on the chart (see page 145 for how to work French knots) and then repeat the motif at each side, placing each center line of the motif 42 intersections away from the main center line. Remove the tacking (basting) stitches and lightly press on the wrong side to finish.

A hundred thousand welcomes:

Coriolanus, Act II, scene 4

SHAKESPEARE

'WELCOME TO MY KITCHEN' SAMPLER

A good cook is like a sorceress who dispenses happiness.

Shocking Life,

ELSA SCHIAPARELLI

In most households the kitchen is often thought of as 'the heart of the home'. I know I like to think that my kitchen, with its casual coziness, is not only a place where meals are planned and produced but where all members of the family and friends feel welcome to sit and linger awhile.

My inspiration for this design came directly from the traditional samplers of the nineteenth century, especially those depicting a religious or moral motto surrounded by a pretty, decorative border. These were usually worked by young girls eager to practice new stitches and patterns they had learned. It was then currently fashionable to work individual words in different colors which strikes me today as a fairly modern approach to design .

The finished unframed sampler measures 32 cm × 30 cm (12½ in × 12 in)

✐ MATERIALS

40 cm (16 in) square of antique brown linen,
  19 threads to 2.5 cm (1 in)
Tacking (basting) thread
Tapestry needle size 22
Embroidery frame (optional)
DMC 6-strand embroidery floss: see the thread list
  on the right
32 cm × 30 cm(12½ × 12 in) of 3 mm (⅛ in)
  cardboard for mounting the sampler
32 cm × 30 cm(12½ × 12 in) of lightweight
  synthetic wadding (batting)
Strong thread or masking tape for securing the
  mounted embroidery
Picture frame of your choice

✐ THREAD LIST

783	yellow	606	red
776	pale pink	471	pale green
760	pink	700	green
309	deep pink	991	deep green

✐ THE EMBROIDERY

Mark the center of your fabric both ways with tacking (basting) stitches and stretch the fabric in a frame, if preferred (see page 143). Alternatively, provided you work with an even tension, this weight of linen can be worked in the hand.

Following the color key and the chart, where one square is equal to one stitch worked over two threads of fabric, begin the embroidery by backstitching the central horizontal line working outwards from the middle and using three strands of thread, deep pink 309, in the needle. Use three strands for all the backstitched lines, including the two hearts, and two strands for the main embroidery.

Complete the embroidery beginning and finishing threads underneath existing stitches. Work without carrying threads across the back of the sampler, to prevent them from showing through on the right side.

Lightly steam-press the finished embroidery on the wrong side.

Mount and frame the completed embroidery following the instructions on page 148.

CHAPTER

3

—

HOLIDAYS
AND
CELEBRATIONS

Easter

Fair vernal flowers, laugh forth
Your ancient gladness!
Christ is risen.

An Easter Hymn,
THOMAS BLACKBURN

EASTER GREETING CARD

Christ being raised from the dead dieth no more:
death hath no more dominion over him.

Romans VI, Verse 9

The giving of eggs at Easter time is an old custom – they were originally given in Spring time as a symbol of fertility, birth and growth but later became synonymous with the Resurrection.

All kinds of eggs – ranging from dyed and painted birds' eggs to those carved from wood or made from chocolate – are still exchanged between families and friends around the world. And what better way to celebrate Easter than to send your greetings with a pretty card you have embroidered yourself.

The finished greeting card measures overall 20 cm × 14 cm (8 in × 5½ in) with a cut-out measuring 14 cm × 9.5 cm (5½ in × 3¾ in)

MATERIALS

23 cm × 18 cm (9 in × 7 in) of white Aida fabric, 13 threads to 2.5 cm (1 in)
Tacking (basting) thread
Tapestry needle size 24
Embroidery hoop (optional)
DMC 6-strand embroidery floss: see the thread list on the right
Card mount with oval cut-out (see page 157 for suppliers)

THREAD LIST

744	pale yellow	794	light blue
729	old gold	799	blue
747	pale turquoise	818	pink
597	deep turquoise	3354	mid pink
472	lime green	3733	deep pink
372	khaki	3350	dark red

THE EMBROIDERY

Mark the center of the fabric both ways with tacking (basting) stitches. Work in a hoop or in the hand, as preferred (see page 142).

Following the color key and chart, where each square is equal to one stitch worked over one intersection of fabric, begin the cross stitching in the center. Use two strands of thread in the needle and complete the embroidery, working outwards from the middle. Finish by working the stems in backstitch using khaki 372, and then outline the bow with deep turquoise 597. Similarly, outline the remaining ribbon and the picot edging.

Retain the tacking (basting) stitches, steam-press on the wrong side and mount the card following the instructions given for Birthday Greeting Cards on page 16.

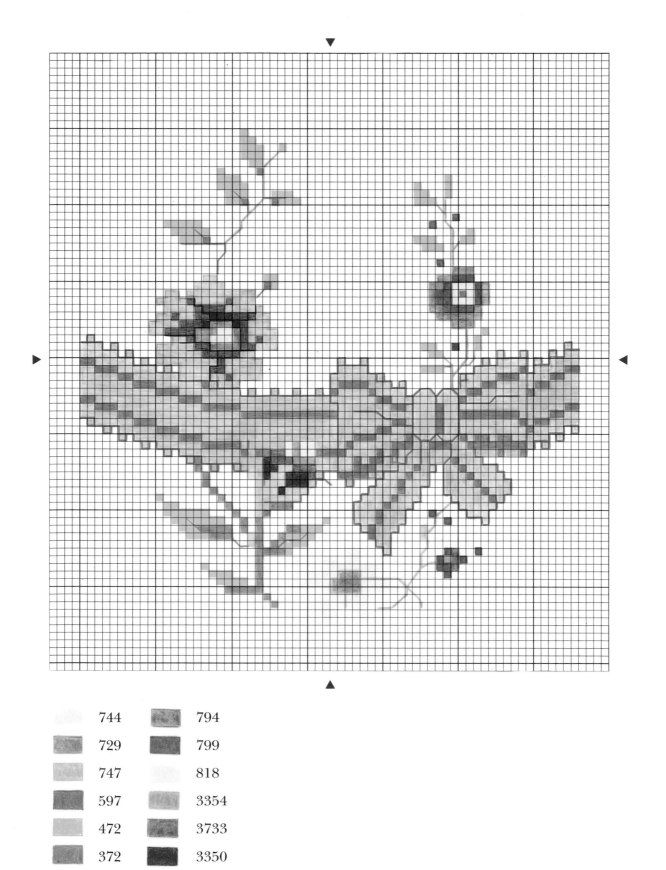

744   794

729   799

747   818

597   3354

472   3733

372   3350

EASTER EGG BASKET LINER

When my children were young, my table decoration at Easter time was a large straw-lined basket (nest) filled with chocolate and marzipan eggs. My sons added real birds' feathers to the straw and perched models of lifelike birds on top. While feathers and birds may not be to everyone's taste, I know how most children enjoy edible Easter eggs.

A simple basket of eggs with a pretty liner makes a very attractive table setting for this festive occasion. Eggs to eat can be painted or dyed hens' eggs, marzipan or foil-wrapped chocolate varieties. At Easter, some confectioners make sweets to resemble birds' eggs. These come in soft colors with spotted and plain surfaces – the ideal complement for this pastel-colored liner.

The finished liner measures 30 cm × 30 cm (12 in × 12 in)

☞ MATERIALS

38 cm (15 in) square of white Aida fabric, 13 threads to 2.5 cm (1 in)
Tacking (basting) thread
Tapestry needle size 24
Embroidery hoop (optional)
DMC 6-strand embroidery floss: see the thread list below
Tracing paper
15 cm (6 in) square of thin cardboard (cereal box)
Contrast bias binding, 12 mm (½ in) wide, and matching sewing thread

☞ THREAD LIST

3047	buff	907	grass green
726	yellow	3024	pale grey
742	deep golden yellow	3713	pale pink
841	brown	3688	pink
472	pale green		

☞ THE EMBROIDERY

Mark the center of the Aida fabric both ways with tacking (basting) stitches. Work in a hoop (see page 142) or in the hand, as preferred. Following the color key and chart, where each square represents one cross stitch worked over one intersection of fabric, begin the embroidery with the rabbit motif. Use two strands of thread in the

'Twas Easter Sunday, The full blossomed trees
Filled all the air with fragrance and with joy.

The Spanish Student,
H W LONGFELLOW

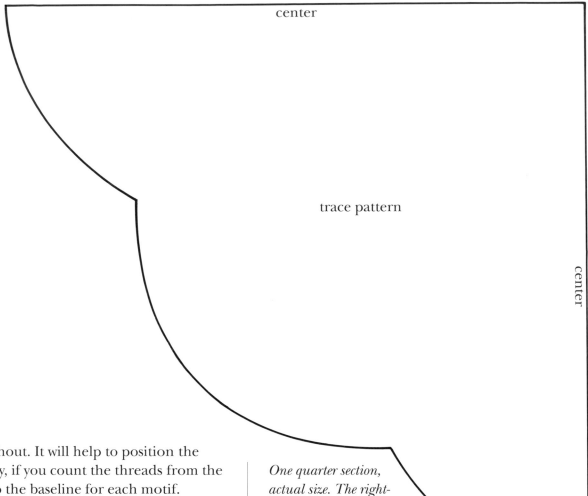

center

trace pattern

center

needle throughout. It will help to position the motifs correctly, if you count the threads from the center down to the baseline for each motif. Complete the rabbits and then turn your embroidery through 90° to work the ducklings. Complete the remaining motifs in the same way. Lightly press on the wrong side but retain the tacking (basting) stitches.

One quarter section, actual size. The right-hand vertical line and the top horizontal line match the center lines of the embroidery.

☞ SHAPING THE EDGE

Trace the outline of the quarter section given above, using a soft pencil. Transfer it to the cardboard: place the tracing on the card, pencil side down, and go over the outline. Cut out the template. Lay the embroidery right side down on a clean surface and place the template over one quarter section, matching the tacked (basted) lines. Lightly draw around the scalloped edge, then repeat in the remaining quarter sections. Cut out the shape and remove the tacking (basting) stitches.

☞ BINDING THE EDGE

With the right sides together, pin and tack (baste) the bias binding around the edge (see page 147). Beginning in the corner of a scallop, turn the raw edge over to the wrong side, to neaten. Ease the binding around the curves and the inside angles and overlap the two ends by 6 mm (¼ in). Either machine-stitch in place or backstitch by hand.

Turn the binding over the edge to the wrong side and, using matching sewing thread, hem around, stitching into the previous stitches to prevent them from showing through.

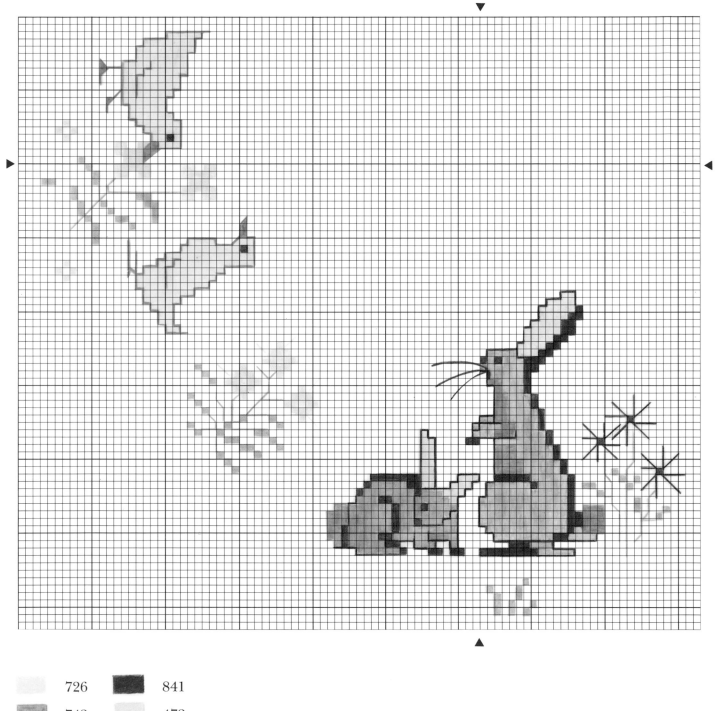

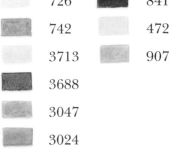

726   841

742   472

3713   907

3688

3047

3024

Thanksgiving

O give thanks unto the Lord, for he is good:
for His mercy endureth for ever.

Psalms 107, Verse 1

THANKSGIVING PLACE MAT

*There is nothing more rewarding than to see a handsomely dressed
dining table giving a festive welcome to visiting family and friends.
Thanksgiving is the autumnal occasion in North America when thanks
are given in celebration of the Early Settlers' first harvest, I chose
contrasting fruits of late summer to decorate this colorful place mat,
which you can repeat to make a set.*

The finished place mat measures 36 cm × 30 cm
(14 in × 12 in)

⌒ MATERIALS
36 cm × 30 cm (14 in × 12 in) of pale khaki Aida
    fabric, 16 threads to 2.5 cm (1 in)
Tacking (basting) thread
Tapestry needle size 26
Embroidery hoop (optional)
DMC 6-strand embroidery floss: see the thread list
    overleaf

*Without Thy sunshine and Thy rain
We could not have the golden grain;
Without Thy Love we'd not be fed'
We thank Thee for our daily bread.*

Anon

744	
743	
3348	
702	
3032	
611	
776	
3733	
350	
327	
823	

☞ THREAD LIST

744	pale yellow		327	purple
743	yellow		832	dark blue
776	pale pink		611	brown
3733	pink		3032	light brown
3348	grass green		350	red
702	green			

☞ THE EMBROIDERY

To position the design in the lower left corner of
the fabric, first mark a rectangle on the Aida
fabric in tacking (basting) stitches, placing it 5 cm
(2 in) in from the outside edges. Work in a hoop
(see page 142) or in the hand, as preferred.

Following the color key and the chart, where
each square is equal to one stitch worked over one
intersection of fabric, begin the cross stitching
working outwards from the corner in both
directions using two strands of thread in the
needle. Complete the embroidery, adding the
backstitch details last. Using green thread 702,
complete the rectangular border.

Trim the edges of the fabric, if needed, and
lightly steam-press on the wrong side. Still using
green thread 702, hem-stitch around the mat about
12 mm (½ in) in from the raw edge (see page 145
for how to hem-stitch). Make each hem-stitch two
thread intersections across and two deep.

Fringe the edges by removing the fabric threads
up to the hem-stitching.

PRESERVE POT COVERS

Stands the Church clock at ten to three?

And is there honey still for tea?

The Old Vicarage, Granchester,

RUPERT BROOKE

I*n my family, jams, jellies, marmalades, chutneys and pickles are made throughout the year, whenever fruits and vegetables are in season. As a child, I enjoyed cutting out colorful pictures of fruits from glossy magazines and sticking them onto my mother's preserve jars, but now I have a wonderful range of pot covers stitched with deliciously enticing fruits and vegetables – kept just for the pots in current use. These washable pot covers also make excellent gifts – with or without the jars and their contents.*

Each finished preserve pot cover measures 18 cm (7 in) across, with a 6.5 cm (2½ in) central circle of Hardanger fabric

☞ MATERIALS

Three lace-edged pot covers with cream
   evenweave centres, 18 threads to 2.5 cm (1 in)
   (see page 157 for suppliers)
Tacking (basting) thread
Tapestry needle size 26
Embroidery hoop (optional)
DMC 6-strand embroidery floss: see the thread
   lists on the right
2.1 m (2⅓ yds) of bright yellow satin ribbon,
   6 mm (¼ in) wide
Ribbon threader

☞ THREAD LISTS

Apples

744	pale yellow	3341	deep apricot
725	yellow	350	red
472	light green	730	brown
907	green		

Strawberries

445	pale yellow	797	royal blue
725	yellow	992	viridian green
224	strawberry pink	954	green
350	red	3012	olive green
316	rose pink	991	dark green
3328	deep pink		

Cherries

962	pink	605	vermilion
3350	deep pink	964	peppermint green
327	purple	958	viridian green
760	salmon pink	792	deep blue
309	red		

☞ THE EMBROIDERY

All three covers are embroidered in the same way, using two strands of thread in the needle throughout. Mark the center of the evenweave fabric both ways with tacking (basting) stitches and stretch it in a hoop, if preferred (see page 142). However, since there is little embroidery, you may prefer to work in your hand.

Following the appropriate color key and chart, where one square is equal to one cross stitch, embroider the design, working outwards from the middle. In each case, complete the cross stitching and then work the backstitching last of all. Remove the tacking (basting) threads.

Cut the ribbon into three equal lengths and thread it through the holes in the lace edging of each cover, using the ribbon threader.

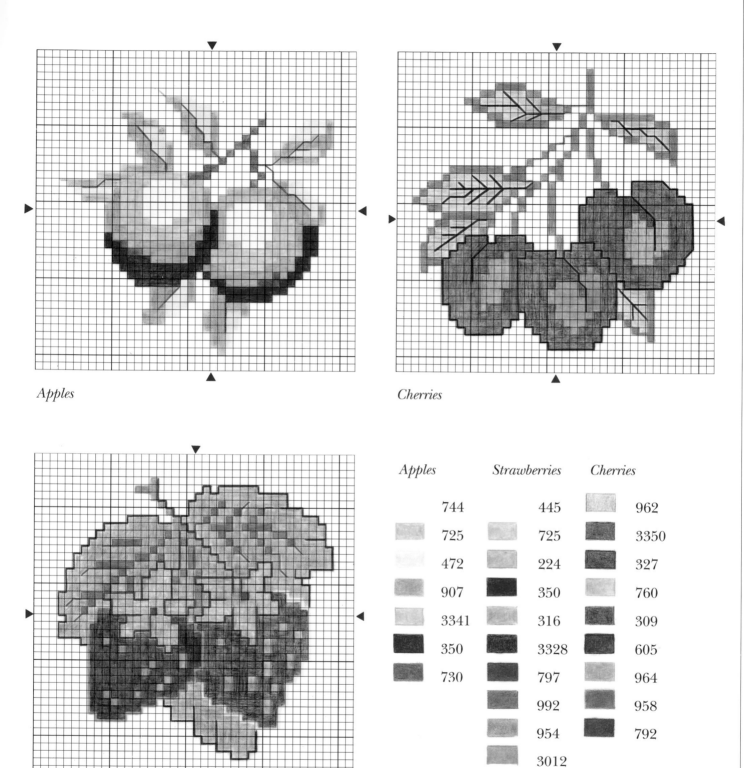

Apples

Cherries

Strawberries

Apples		Strawberries		Cherries	
	744		445		962
	725		725		3350
	472		224		327
	907		350		760
	3341		316		309
	350		3328		605
	730		797		964
			992		958
			954		792
			3012		
			991		

Christmas

This most tremendous tale of all,
Seen in a stained-glass window's hue,
A baby in an ox's stall.

Christmas,

JOHN BETJEMAN

CHRISTMAS STOCKINGS

The little red stockings he silently fills,
Till the stockings will hold no more;
The bright little sleds for the great snow hills
Are quickly set down on the floor.
Then Santa Claus mounts to the roof like a bird,
And glides to his seat in the sleigh;
Not the sound of a bugle or drum is heard
As he noiselessly gallops away.

Santa Claus,
TRADITIONAL

*T*he delightful custom of children hanging up a stocking on Christmas Eve ready for Santa Claus's arrival is thought to have begun with the story of Saint Nicholas (Father Christmas). Legend tells how a father was unable to provide dowries for his three daughters so, one night, Saint Nicholas threw purses of gold through the house window and they were caught in stockings which had been left to dry by the fire.

Today, we like to fill our children's stockings with lots of small gifts, aiming to keep them occupied until larger gifts are opened later in the day. You may wish to work the recipient's name or initials into the design so the child will always have his or her own very special stocking ready at Christmas time.

The finished stockings measures 30 cm × 13 cm (12 in × 5 in)

☞ MATERIALS

For each stocking

18 cm × 10 cm (7 in × 4 in) of white Aida fabric, 18 threads to 2.5 cm (1 in)

Tacking (basting) thread

Tapestry needle size 26

Small embroidery hoop (optional)

DMC 6-strand embroidery floss: see the thread list on the right

Dressmaker's graph paper

38 cm (15 in) square of contrast cotton fabric for the lining

38 cm (15 in) square of lightweight synthetic wadding (batting)

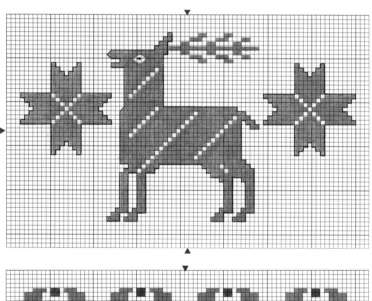

606

992

Reindeer stocking

38 cm (15 in) square of green cotton fabric

Red cotton bias binding, 12 mm (½ in) wide

Noël stocking

38 cm (15 in) square of red cotton fabric

Green cotton bias binding, 12 mm (½ in) wide

☞ THREAD LIST

606

992

606   red
992   green
white

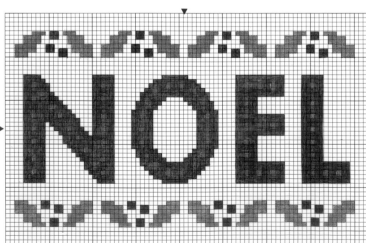

☞ THE EMBROIDERY

Both stockings are embroidered and made in the same way. Mark the center of the Aida fabric both ways with tacking (basting) stitches. Work in a small hoop or in the hand, as preferred (see page 142).

Following the color key and the appropriate chart, where each square represents one stitch worked over one intersection of fabric, begin the embroidery in the center, using two strands of thread in the needle. Complete the cross stitching and outline the reindeer and stars in backstitch using red thread. Remove the tacking (basting) stitches and lightly steam-press on the wrong side.

☞ MAKING THE STOCKING

Enlarge the stocking pattern pieces below onto dressmaker's graph paper (see page 143) and cut

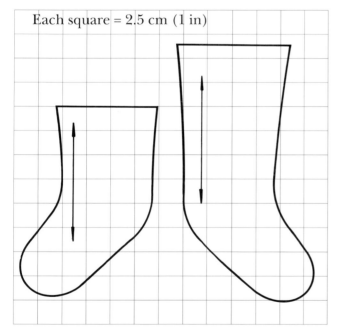

Each square = 2.5 cm (1 in)

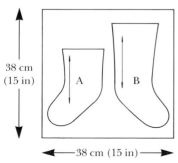

38 cm
(15 in)

A   B

← 38 cm (15 in) →

CUTTING LAYOUT
A – front stocking
cut 1
B – back stocking
cut 1

out the two pattern pieces as instructed in the diagram left. Cut out the stocking from red or green fabric. Using the back stocking pattern piece, cut out two pieces from the lining fabric and two from the wadding (batting) and put them to one side.

Trim the edges of the embroidered front band to measure 15 cm × 8.5 cm (6 in × 3¼ in). Cover the bottom edge with bias binding (see page 147). Join the band to the front stocking section: with both pieces right side up, pin the band over the top raw edge of the stocking and machine-stitch across through the edge of the binding.

Assemble the layers for the two stocking sections as follows: place the lining wrong side up, the wadding (batting) next and then the top fabric right side up: trim the top band to size, shaping the sides outwards. Pin the layers together and, using white 6-strand embroidery floss, work large French knots (see page 145) at random over the surface to hold the layers secure. Tack (baste) around the edges of both pieces. Cover the top edge of both sections with bias binding.

Place the two pieces together, right sides out, then pin and tack (baste) around the edge. Cover the raw edges with bias binding. To make a loop at the top edge, extend the binding by about 13 cm (5 in) and machine the edges together along with the final stitching. Fold into a loop and hand-stitch to the top inside edge.

CHRISTMAS TREE ORNAMENTS

Long before shiny baubles and tinsel were invented, it was customary to decorate the Christmas tree with handmade ornaments and toys. These would include a range of miniature toys – often painted wooden dolls for girls and animals for boys – as well as simple cookies and sweets carefully molded and placed in pretty baskets or containers of some kind, to be eaten by the children over the festive period.

Preparing for Christmas is always exciting, and decorating the tree is a special event in most households. Each year we unwrap our treasured heirlooms and add new decorations to our collection. You could add one or two of the cross-stitched ornaments to an existing collection or begin a new one using just one of the motifs, such as the star or sweet-filled cone decorated with a cupid, for example. Children love them!

I heard the bells on Christmas Day
Their old familiar carols play,
And wild and sweet
The words repeat
Of peace on earth, goodwill to men!

Christmas Bells,

H W LONGFELLOW

⌐ MATERIALS

Star

The finished star measures 10 cm × 10 cm
(4 in × 4 in)

Two 15 cm (6 in) squares of white Aida fabric,
    13 threads to 2.5 cm (1 in)
Tacking (basting) thread
Tapestry needle size 24
Small embroidery hoop (optional)
DMC 6-strand embroidery floss: see the thread list
    on page 115
Tracing paper
Two 10 cm (4 in) squares of thin cardboard
Two 10 cm (4 in) squares of lightweight wadding
    (batting)
Masking tape
80 cm (31 in) of 3 mm (⅛ in) wide red ribbon
Fabric glue
One red bead, 1 cm (⅜ in) across

Snowman

The finished snowman measures 13 cm × 8 cm
(5 in × 3 in)

Two 18 cm × 13 cm (7 in × 5 in) pieces of white
    Aida fabric, 13 threads to 2.5 cm (1 in)
Tacking (basting) thread
Tapestry needle size 24
Small embroidery hoop (optional)
DMC 6-strand embroidery floss: see the thread list
    on page 115
Tracing paper
Two 13 cm × 8 cm (5 in × 3 in) pieces of thin
    cardboard
Two 13 cm × 8 cm (5 in × 3 in) pieces of
    lightweight wadding (batting)
Masking tape
80 cm (31 in) of 3 mm (⅛ in) wide deep blue
    ribbon
Fabric glue
One blue bead, 1 cm (⅜ in) across

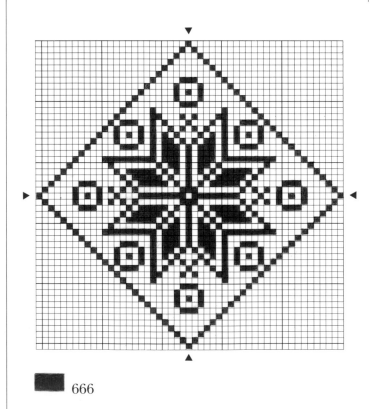

666

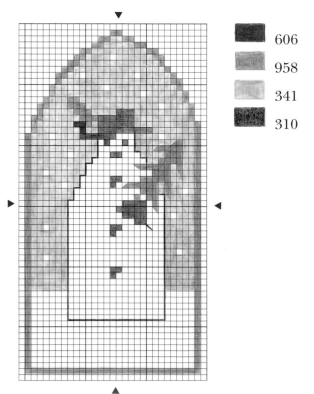

606
958
341
310

Angel

The finished angel measures 10 cm × 10 cm
(4 in × 4 in)

Two 15 cm (6 in) squares of white Aida fabric,
    13 threads to 2.5 cm (1 in)
Tacking (basting) thread
Tapestry needle size 24
Small embroidery hoop (optional)
DMC Light gold metallic thread
27 tiny gold beads
One white bead, 1 cm (³⁄₈ in) across
Tracing paper
Two 10 cm (4 in) squares of thin cardboard
Two 10 cm (4 in) squares of lightweight wadding
    (batting)
Masking tape
1 m (40 in) of 3 mm (¹⁄₈ in) wide gold ribbon or
    Russia braid
Fabric glue
One metal bell, 1 cm (³⁄₈ in) across

Cone with cupid

The finished cone measures 14 cm × 9 cm
(5½ in × 3½ in)

23 cm × 17 cm (9 in × 6½ in) of green Aida fabric,
    13 threads to 2.5 cm (1 in)
Tacking (basting) thread
23 cm × 17 cm (9 in × 6½ in) of contrast cotton
    fabric for the lining
DMC 6-strand embroidery floss: see the thread list
    on page 115
Tapestry needle size 24
Contrasting bias binding, 12 mm (½ in) wide
Matching sewing thread

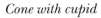

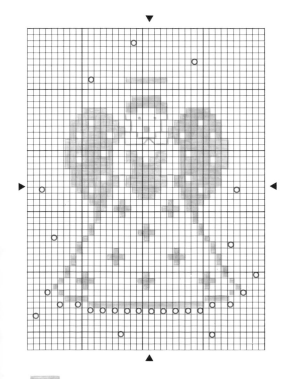

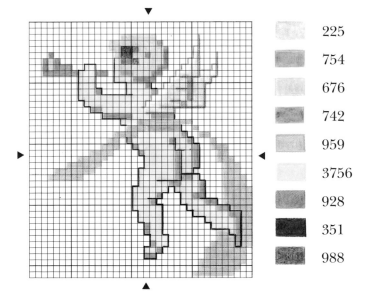

	225
	754
	676
	742
	959
	3756
	928
	351
	988

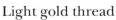 Light gold thread

○ Gold beads

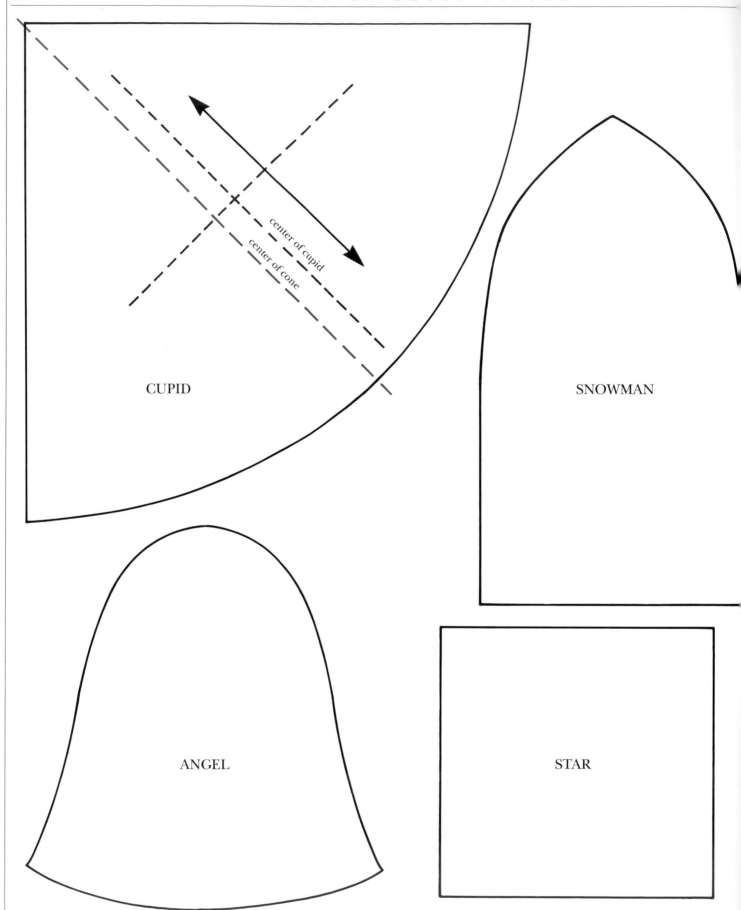

center of cupid

center of cone

CUPID

SNOWMAN

ANGEL

STAR

Star
666   red

Snowman
| 606 | red | 341 | blue |
| 958 | viridian green | 310 | black |

Angel
DMC light gold metallic thread

Cone with cupid
225	flesh	3756	pale grey
754	salmon pink	928	grey
676	gold	351	red
742	yellow	988	green
959	viridian green		

☞ THE EMBROIDERY

All four ornaments are embroidered in the same way. Begin by marking the center of your fabric both ways with tacking (basting) stitches. Work in a small hoop if you wish, but as long as you keep an even tension, small amounts of embroidery, such as these, can be worked in the hand without much risk of pulling the fabric out of shape.

Following the appropriate color key and chart, where each square is equal to one stitch, work the cross stitch outwards from the middle using two strands of thread in the needle. Finish the cross stitching and then add the backstitching last.

For the angel, attach gold beads as indicated on the chart (see page 144 for sewing on beads).

☞ MAKING UP THE ORNAMENTS
Star, Snowman and Angel
Transfer the outline given to the card. Either trace it and place the tracing pencil side down on the card and go over the outline, or photocopy the page and cut out the shape which you can then place on the card, draw around and cut out. Using this as a template, cut out the two pieces of wadding (batting).

Assemble the three layers: put the wadding

(batting) on the card with the embroidery on top, right side up. Secure the fabric edges to the back of the card with masking tape. Cover the second piece of card in the same way. With the front and back sections together, overcast the edges. Cover the edge with the ribbon, attaching it with a thin coating of fabric glue. Apart from the angel, finish with a loop on top and then thread on a bead to cover the join. Knot above to hold (see the diagram right).

For the angel, begin sticking on the gold ribbon at the center bottom edge, leaving a tail of about 8 cm (3 in). Continue as before, finishing at the center bottom and leaving a matching tail. At the top, stitch the two ribbons together to form a loop and attach the bell with a knot to the bottom.

Cone with cupid
Trace the quarter circle (opposite) and add a 1 cm (⅜ in) seam allowance to both straight edges, and cut out.

Place the pattern on your embroidery with the center lines matching, and cut out. Cut out the lining fabric to the same shape. Put the two fabrics wrong sides together and treat as one. Cover the curved edge with bias binding (see page 147).

With the right side inside, place the two straight edges together and machine-stitch to secure. Trim the seam back to 6 mm (¼ in) and zigzag stitch the raw edge to neaten. Turn through to the right side.

To make a hanging loop from bias binding, cut a length of about 30 cm (12 in) and stitch the two folded edges together. Turn under the short edges and attach to the cone, covering the seam with one end and placing the other at the opposite side. Hem in place with matching sewing thread.

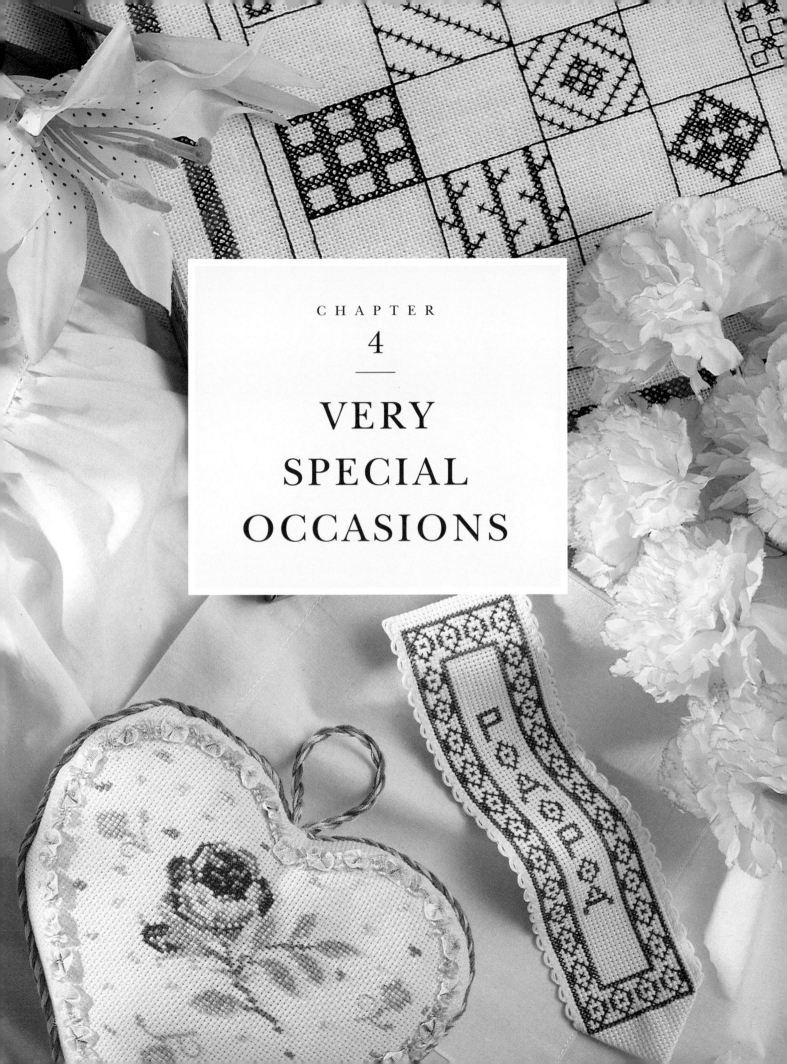

CHAPTER

4

—

VERY
SPECIAL
OCCASIONS

St Valentine's Day

Two souls with but a single thought,
Two hearts that beat as one.

Ingomar the Barbarian II,
MARIA LOVELL

HEART-SHAPED PILLOW

Come live with me, and be my love;
And we will all the pleasures prove.

The Passionate Shepherdess to his Love,

CHRISTOPHER MARLOWE

The delightful custom of giving red roses to a loved one on St Valentine's Day was the inspiration for this simple heart-shaped pillow. Such a gift might be exchanged between sisters, mother and daughter or friends, for example as a token of their love and friendship for each other.

The giving of red roses during courtship, however, is thought to have been started by Louis XVI of France who gave them to his queen, Marie Antoinette.

The finished pillow measures 18 cm × 15 cm (7 in × 6 in)

⌐ MATERIALS

23 cm (9 in) square of pale blue Aida fabric, 16 threads to 2.5 cm (1 in)
Tacking (basting) thread
Tapestry needle size 26
Embroidery hoop (optional)
DMC 6-strand embroidery floss: see the thread list below
Tracing paper
23 cm (9 in) square of pale blue lining fabric
60 cm (24 in) of floral trim, 12 mm (½ in) wide
Matching sewing threads
Loose wadding (batting) for filling pillow
1 m (40 in) of two-color contrast cord

⌐ THREAD LIST

743	yellow
472	pale green
3766	turquoise
907	green
733	olive green
580	dark green
818	pale pink
605	pink
603	deep pink
601	magenta

⌐ THE EMBROIDERY

Mark the center of the Aida fabric both ways with tacking (basting) stitches. Work in a hoop or in the hand, as preferred (see page 142).

Following the color key and the chart, where each square represents one stitch worked over one intersection of fabric, start the embroidery in the center. Use two strands of embroidery thread in the needle and complete the cross stitching, working outwards from the middle. Add the backstitching details last.

Lightly press on the wrong side, if needed.

⌐ MAKING THE PILLOW

Trace the outline given for the heart and draw the second half in reverse. Cut out the template. Pin the tracing on top of the embroidery, matching the center line with the tacking (basting) stitches. Allow an extra 12 mm (½ in) seam allowance all round and cut out. Cut out the lining fabric to the same size.

Sew the floral trim to the pillow front about 12 mm (½ in) in from the seamline, using

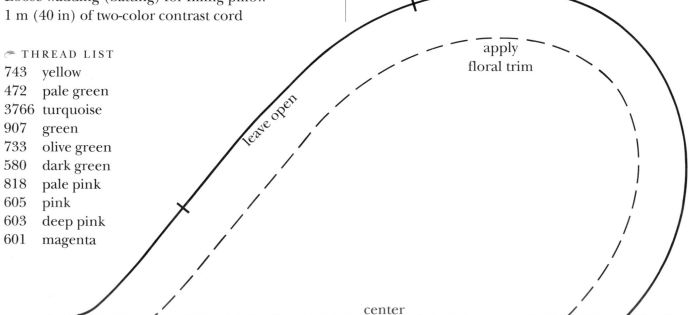

leave open

apply floral trim

center

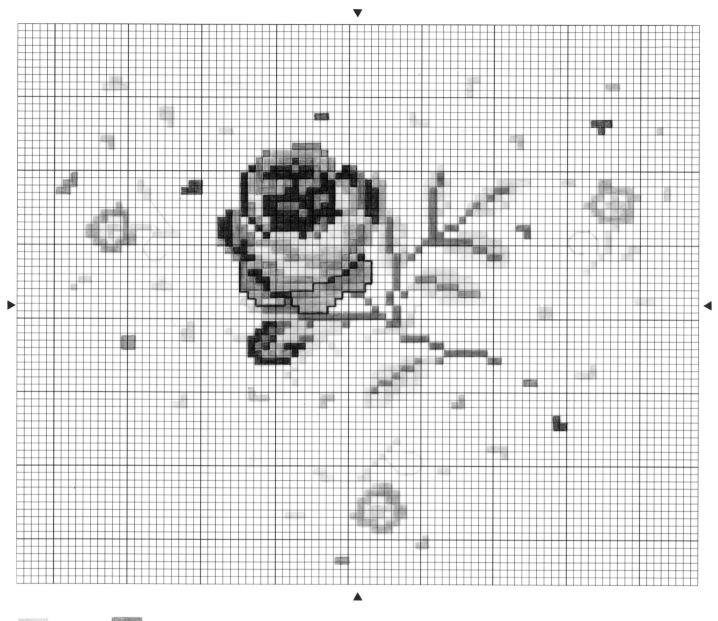

743		580	
472		818	
3766		605	
907		603	
733		601	

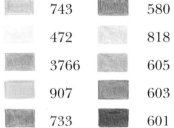

matching thread and small running stitches, making tiny stitches on the right side and larger stitches on the wrong side.

With the right sides inside, pin the two sections together and machine stitch around leaving a small opening in one side, as shown on the trace pattern. Trim the seam, clip into the curves and the inner angle before turning through to the right side. Stuff with loose wadding (batting) to a softly rounded shape. Slipstitch the opening closed.

Cut a 20 cm (8 in) length of cord for the loop, fold in half and slip the ends into the seam at the top of the heart, first snipping the stitches to make a small opening. Attach the cord around the edge following the instructions on page 148.

*S*T *V*ALENTINE'S *D*AY *A*PRON

This old-fashioned muslin hostess apron colorfully stitched with cupids and hearts might be the way to woo a husband or fiancé into the kitchen – especially if there's a delicious meal to prepare. However, such a pretty apron should not be put away until the following Valentine's Day but should, like romance, be a regular feature in a couple's life.
The apron is worn with the shoulder straps crossed over at the back and the ties threaded through the loops, at the end of each strap, before tying in a bow. The length of the straps can be adjusted to fit.

*T*here is no spectacle more appealing than that of a
beautiful women in the act of cooking dinner for
someone she loves.

The Web and the Rock,

THOMAS WOLFE

MATERIALS

The finished apron measures 112 cm (44 in) long

34 cm × 30 cm (13½ in × 12 in) of cream
  Hardanger fabric, 16 threads to 2.5 cm (1 in)
  for the apron bib
Tacking (basting) thread
Tapestry needle size 24
Embroidery hoop
DMC 6-strand embroidery floss: see the thread list
  below
Tracing paper
Dressmaker's carbon paper
Dressmaker's graph paper
Long ruler and colored pencil
1 m (40 in) of 1.5 m (1⅔ yds) wide unbleached
  lightweight muslin
Matching sewing thread
1.85 m (2 yds) of cream broderie anglaise trim,
  5 cm (2 in) wide

THREAD LIST

3756	pale blue	445	pale yellow
928	grey	3348	lime green
3774	flesh	989	green
353	apricot	937	olive green
964	light viridian	3354	pink
959	mid viridian	351	red
676	light gold	958	viridian green
972	deep gold		

THE EMBROIDERY

Mark the center of the evenweave fabric both ways
with tacking (basting) stitches. Working in a hoop
(see page 142), begin the cross stitching in the
middle. Following the color key and chart, where
each square equals one stitch, embroider the
heart then the cupids and the surrounding floral
details, working outwards from the center. Finish
with the outlining, using one strand of red 351 to
outline the cupids, one strand of viridian green
958 to outline the cupids' sashes and two strands
of deep gold 972 to outline the wings.

Trace the double stitched outline of the heart
from the chart and position it over the
embroidery, aligning the center lines with the
tacking (basting) threads. Place the carbon paper
just underneath the border and go over the lines
with pencil. Move the carbon paper along and
repeat the process until the heart is completed.
Avoid marking the existing embroidery with the
carbon paper.

Following the chart, work straight stitches in the
colors shown, using two strands of thread. Retain
the tacking (basting) stitches and steam-press on
the wrong side, if necessary.

CUTTING OUT THE PATTERN PIECES

Enlarge the apron skirt and waistband pattern
pieces on page 126 onto dressmaker's graph
paper (see page 143). Transfer the marks and
instructions and cut out. All seam allowances are
included. Use 1 cm (⅜ in) seams throughout,
unless otherwise given with the instruction for
making up.

Following the cutting layout on page 125, fold
the muslin fabric as indicated and pin the two
pattern pieces in position. Using the ruler and
colored pencil, draw the remaining rectangles
directly onto the fabric as shown in the diagram,
using the following measurements: Shoulder
strap × 4, 90 cm × 6 cm (36 in × 2¼ in); Tie × 2,
86 cm × 14 cm (34 × 5½ in); Pocket × 2, 20 cm ×
26 cm (8 in × 10¼ in); Bib band × 1, 23 cm × 6 cm
(9 in × 2¼ in). Cut out the pattern pieces.

Using the tacking (basting) stitches to keep the
embroidery centered, trim the bib to measure
23 cm × 29.5 cm (9 in × 11½ in). Remove the
tacking (basting) stitches.

MAKING UP THE APRON

On the apron skirt, hem both side edges, first
folding 6 mm (¼ in) and then 1 cm (⅜ in).
Machine-stitch close to the edge.

Neaten the top edge of both pocket pieces, first
folding 1 cm (⅜ in) and then 3.5 cm (1½ in).
Machine-stitch across. On the remaining three
sides, fold under 1 cm (⅜ in) and press. Pin and

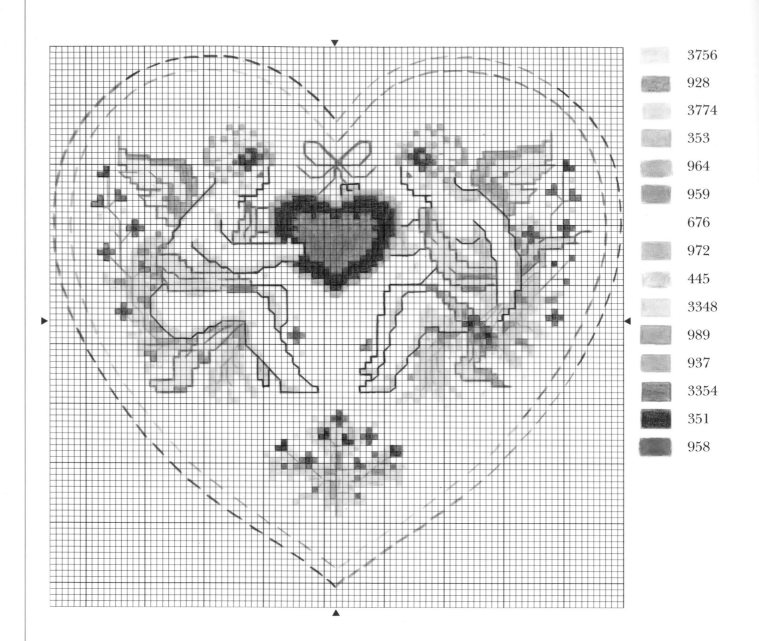

3756
928
3774
353
964
959
676
972
445
3348
989
937
3354
351
958

machine-stitch in the position shown on the pattern, leaving the top edge unstitched but stitching diagonally for 2 cm (¾ in) across the top corners to strengthen them.

On the apron skirt, make a double row of gathering stitches at the waist edge between the points marked. Pull up the gathers to fit the curved edge of the waistband. With the right side of one waistband section to the wrong side of the apron waist edge and leaving the short edges extending beyond the apron by 1 cm (⅜ in), pin and machine-stitch in place. This becomes the underside of the waistband. Put to one side.

On the apron ties, make double 6 mm (¼ in) hems along the long edges and machine-stitch. Neaten one short side with a 1 cm (⅜ in) double fold. Pleat the opposite short side to fit the waistband.

On the waistband, fold in the extended seam allowance and tack (baste) the pleated tie in place. Repeat on the opposite side.

With the right sides together, pin the bib band to the top edge of the bib, raw edges matching, and machine-stitch, taking a 3 cm (1¼ in) seam. Press the band upwards, make a narrow hem on the raw edge and slipstitch to the wrong side.

Cut the broderie anglaise trim in half and pin one piece to one section of shoulder strap, leaving 18 cm (7 in) untrimmed at one end of each strap. Taper each end of the trim by angling it into the seam allowance. If there is a right and wrong side to the broderie anglaise, make sure you trim a right and left hand shoulder strap. Machine-stitch within the seam allowance. Pin a second strap section on top of the trim and then machine-stitch the long edge through all layers. Turn to the right side so that the trim is now on the outside edge of each strap and press.

Join the straps to the bib. With the right sides together, pin and stitch the appropriate strap to the side of the bib, beginning at the waist edge. Repeat on the opposite side. Press the seam and turn the underside of the strap over to the wrong side. Turn under the raw edge and tack (baste) in

place. Turn in the raw edges of the remaining strap, tack (baste) and machine-stitch along the whole length, including the side of the bib, and stitching from the right side. Make a loop at the end of each shoulder strap to carry the waist tie. Fold under about 6.5 cm (2½ in) and machine-stitch across.

With the wrong sides together, pin and tack (baste) the bib centrally to the apron waistband. Tack (baste) the second waistband section on top of the bib, right sides together, and stitch across. Turn the waistband to the right side, press the seam towards the waistband and then make single hems on all the remaining raw edges. Tack (baste) in place covering the ties on the short sides of the band. Working from the right side, machine-stitch around the short sides and the curved edge of the waistband to secure.

Make a 6.5 cm (2½ in) hem on the lower edge of the apron and stitch across, continuing the stitching down the sides of the hem to finish.

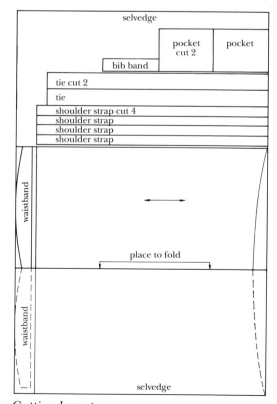

Cutting layout

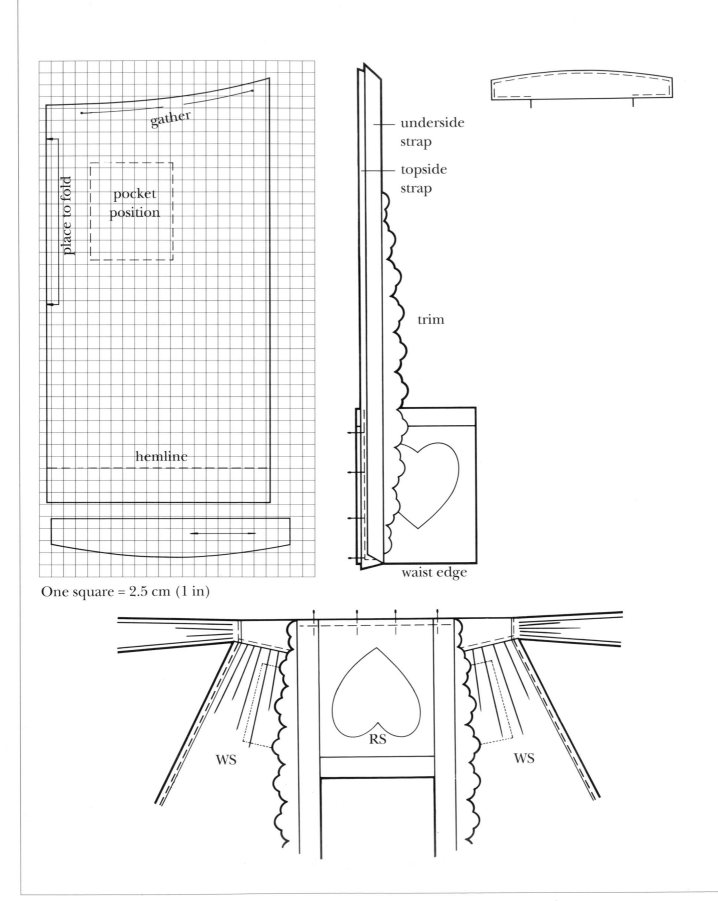

gather

place to fold

pocket
position

hemline

One square = 2.5 cm (1 in)

underside
strap

topside
strap

trim

waist edge

WS   RS   WS

Mother's Day

Who ran to help me when I fell,
And would some pretty story tell,
Or kiss the place to make it well?
My mother.

My Mother,
ANN TAYLOR

SLEEP PILLOW

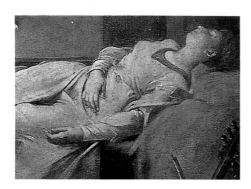

Aheadrest filled with sweet-smelling herbs makes an ideal present for Mother's Day. One of my favorite fillings is a mixture of rose petals and a few drops of lavender oil. These fillings are placed in a muslin bag before stitching it into the pillow cover, to prevent the crushed herbs from eventually coming through the cover in a powdery form. Openweave fabrics, such as Aida, are ideal for allowing the scent to permeate through.

Interestingly, fragrant sleep-inducing stuffings go back to medieval times when mattresses were filled with straw and herbs – some herbs being appropriately named, such as Lady's Bedstraw.

The finished pillow measures 24 cm × 22 cm (9½ in × 8½ in)

✎ MATERIALS
33 cm × 30 cm (13 in × 12 in) of cream Aida
    fabric, 14 threads to 2.5 cm (1 in)
Tacking (basting) thread
Tapestry needle size 24
Embroidery hoop (optional)
DMC 6-strand embroidery floss: see the thread list
    on the right
27 cm × 24 cm (10½ in × 9½ in) of cream cotton
    backing fabric
Matching sewing threads

Two 27 cm × 24 cm (10½ in × 9½ in) pieces of
    white muslin
Sufficient sweet-smelling herbs, rose petals and
    lavender oil or potpourri to fill the pillow
27 cm × 24 cm (10½ in × 9½ in) cushion pad
    (optional)
1.5 m (60 in) of two-color contrast cord,
    6 mm (¼ in) across
Medium size sewing needle

✎ THREAD LIST

772	lime green	3042	mauve
445	lemon yellow	224	apricot
726	yellow	3354	pale pink
471	green	3688	pink
976	grey green	3687	deep pink

✎ THE EMBROIDERY
Mark the center of the Aida fabric both ways with the tacking (basting) stitches. Work in a hoop or in the hand, as preferred (see page 142).

Following the color key and chart, where each square represents one stitch worked over one thread intersection, begin the embroidery working outwards from the center, using two strands of thread in the needle. Complete the cross stitching and finish by working the backstitch details on top. Retain the tacking (basting) stitches, and lightly steam-press the finished embroidery on the wrong side.

Oh sleep! it is a gentle thing,
    Beloved from pole to pole!

The Rime of the Ancient Mariner,
SAMUEL TAYLOR COLERIDGE

☞ MAKING THE PILLOW

Should the edges of the Aida fabric have frayed, use the tacking (basting) stitches to trim the edges evenly, keeping the embroidery centered, then trim further to the size of the backing fabric.

Place the front and back sections right sides together, tack (baste) and machine-stitch around, taking a 12 mm (½ in) seam and leaving a 15 cm (6 in) opening along one long edge. Trim across the corners and turn the cover through to the right side.

Make the muslin bag as for the outer cover, loosely fill with your chosen scented filling and then machine-stitch the opening together. Alternatively, insert the cushion pad, turn under the raw edges of the opening and slipstitch to close, leaving a 2 cm (¾ in) gap. Attach the cord around the edge following the instructions on page 148.

☞ TASSELS

These very simple tassels are made from the remaining cord. Cut four 8 cm (3 in) lengths. Fold one piece in half and, using matching sewing thread, attach it to a corner of the pillow, stitching it through the center. Fold the cord and, with the thread, bind around close to the stitching and fasten off. Untwist the cord and fringe the threads to finish. Repeat on the other three corners of the pillow.

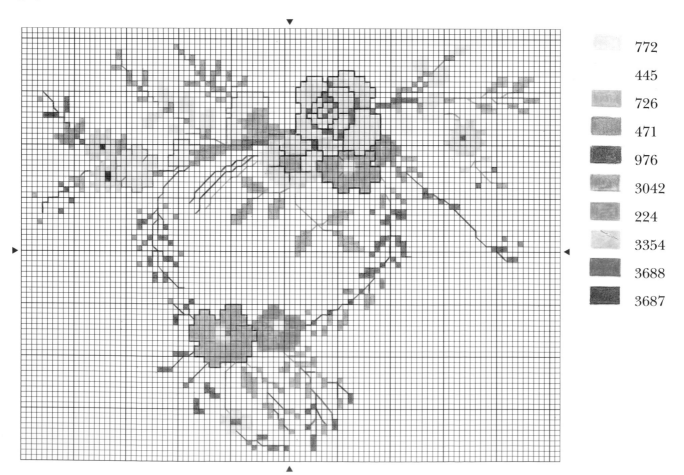

	772
	445
	726
	471
	976
	3042
	224
	3354
	3688
	3687

SCISSORS DOLLY

*I once had a sweet little doll, dears
The prettiest doll in the world.*

The Water Babies,

CHARLES KINGSLEY

*N*o matter how careful we are with our work things, or how many workboxes we have, items can still go astray at the most crucial times. The thing that I seemed to lose most often were my small embroidery scissors but, since I have attached a similar dolly, this no longer happens. Even in an overflowing workbasket, or scattered on a 'busy' work table, either the dolly or the ribbon is usually seen and the scissors are recovered before they got lost.

The dolly is based on the little English lavender dolls, traditionally filled with lavender flowers and placed in chests of drawers to give clothes a lovely lavender fragrance.

The finished dolly measures 10 cm (4 in) high

☞ MATERIALS

23 cm × 15 cm (9 in × 6 in) of white evenweave fabric, 32 threads to 2.5 cm (1 in)
Tacking (basting) thread
Tapestry needle size 26
Embroidery hoop (optional)
DMC 6-strand embroidery floss: see the thread list below
90 cm (36 in) of bright pink ribbon, 3 mm (⅛ in) wide
Matching sewing threads
Loose synthetic wadding (batting)

☞ THREAD LIST

834	light gold	3779	pale pink
725	yellow	899	mid pink
783	deep gold	224	rose pink
472	pale green	3350	deep pink
989	green	598	turquoise blue
992	viridian green		

☞ THE EMBROIDERY

Fold the fabric widthwise in half and tack (baste) the center line, then tack (baste) the center both ways in each section. Stretch the fabric in a hoop, if preferred (see page 142).

Following the appropriate color key and chart, where one square represents two threads of fabric, embroider the design. Using two strands of thread in the needle throughout, work the cross stitching first and then the backstitching. Complete both sections, remove the tacking (basting) threads and steam-press on the wrong side, if necessary.

☞ MAKING UP THE DOLLY

Cut out the front and back pieces, adding a 12 mm (½ in) seam allowance all round. From the narrow ribbon, cut off 15 cm (6 in) and put to one side. Fold the remaining ribbon in half, tack (baste) the cut ends inside the seam allowance at the center top of the front piece, raw edges matching. Pin the loop of ribbon to the center of the fabric on the right side, so that it does not get caught in the seam. With the right sides together and stitched design matching, tack (baste) and machine stitch around the dolly, stitching just inside the embroidery. Leave the base open. Trim the seam, clip into the curved seam and turn through to the right side. Gently stuff with well-teased filling. Turn in the seam allowance at the base and slipstitch to close. Tie the 15 cm (6 in) length of ribbon into a bow and attach it to the top of the head with one or two stitches.

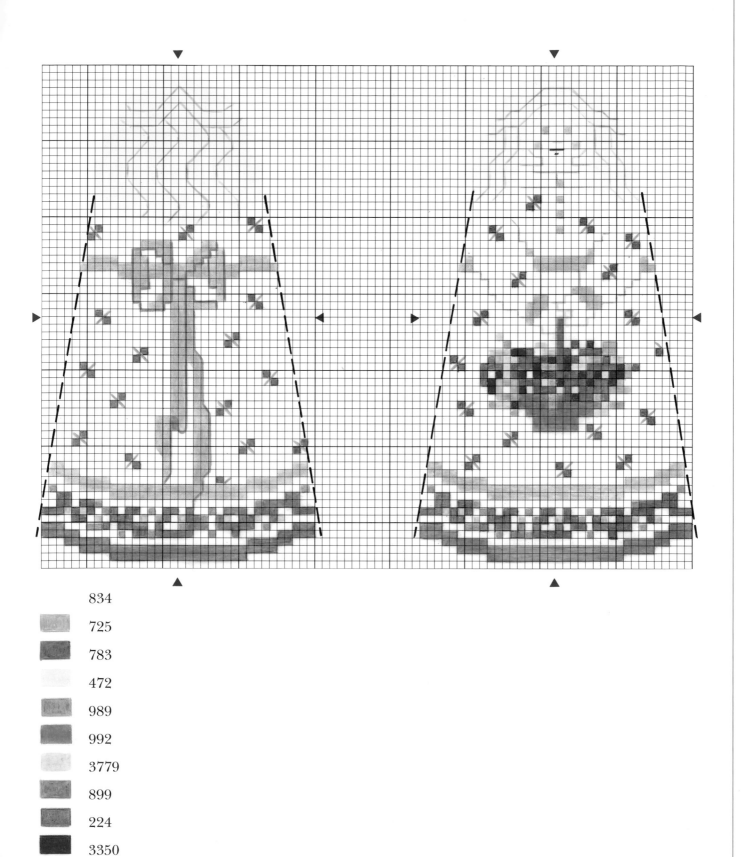

834
725
783
472
989
992
3779
899
224
3350
598

Father's Day

*I have found the happiness of parenthood greater
than any other that I have experienced.*

BERTRAND RUSSELL

CHESSBOARD

*Chess is a sea in which a gnat may drink and
an elephant may bathe.*

Indian proverb

Chess continues to captivate players of all ages. Throughout history, the game has had a spellbinding effect on all who played it and, as long ago as the fifteenth century, contributed to European culture where it was considered a great accomplishment to be a skilled chess player. The actual chess pieces and board (called a chequer) vary enormously in style and shape – and have attracted craftspeople working in all kinds of media from ivory to inlaid silver. This embroidered chessboard, framed under glass, would make a very acceptable gift on Father's Day.

The finished unframed chessboard measures 40 cm (15¾ in) square

☞ MATERIALS

50 cm (20 in) of off-white Zweigart's Cork linen, 19 threads to 2.5 cm (1 in)
Tacking (basting) thread
Tapestry needle size 24
Embroidery hoop or frame
DMC 6-strand embroidery floss: see the thread list below
40 cm (15¾ in) square of 3 mm (⅛ in) cardboard for mounting the embroidery
40 cm (15¾ in) square of lightweight synthetic wadding (batting)
Masking tape or strong thread to secure the mounted embroidery
Frame (with glass) of your choice

☞ THREAD LIST

310   black (four skeins)
347   red (two skeins)

There are rare beauties in chess.

Arab proverb

☞ THE EMBROIDERY

Mark the center of the linen both ways with tacking (basting) stitches. Stretch it in a hoop or frame (see pages 142 and 143) and begin the embroidery by backstitching the lines, working outwards from the center.

All the embroidery, apart from the outer border, is worked in black using two strands of the thread in the needle throughout. Following the chart, where each square represents one stitch worked over two threads of fabric, complete the vertical lines first. Then backstitch the horizontal lines in the same way to form a series of squares.

Fill in alternate squares with the patterns, as shown on the chart. Work the two outer borders to complete one half of the board design and then turn the work around and repeat the design on the opposite side, to complete the embroidery.

Lightly steam-press on the wrong side, and retain the tacking (basting) stitches to help center the embroidery when you mount it on cardboard.

Mount and frame the completed embroidery following the instructions on page 148.

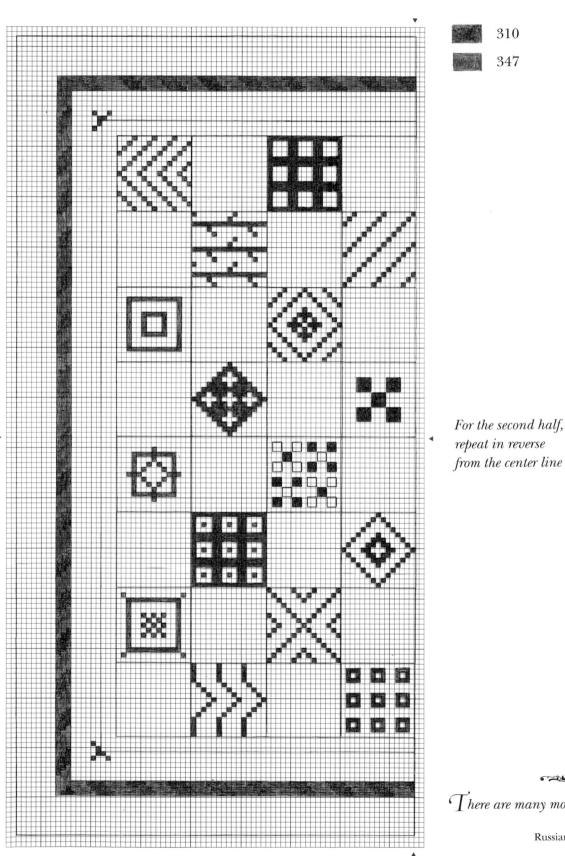

310

347

For the second half,
repeat in reverse
from the center line

There are many moves, but only one mate.

Russian proverb

BOOKMARK

*Knowing how eager many young children are to make their own gifts and
the delight with which they are received, I wanted to include a very easy-to-make
bookmark. This one is worked on a purchased evenweave band, where the
edges are already finished, and the design uses just two colors so that
children can easily substitute their own choice of colors to embroider on a
bookmark as a special present for father.*
The tassel can be omitted, if preferred, and the point left plain and simple.

*A good book is the best of friends, the
same today and for ever.*

Proverbial Philosophy,

MARTIN FARQUHAR TUPPER

The finished bookmark measures 24 cm × 5 cm
(9½ in × 2 in)

⌐ MATERIALS
23 cm (9 in) of cream prepared evenweave band,
    5 cm (2 in) wide, 15 threads to 2.5 cm (1 in)
Tacking (basting) thread
Tapestry needle size 24
DMC 6-strand embroidery floss: see the thread list
    below
Matching sewing thread

⌐ THREAD LIST
347   red   3765 blue

⌐ THE EMBROIDERY
Mark the center of the fabric both ways with
tacking (basting) stitches.

    Working in the hand, follow the color key and
chart, where each square is equal to one stitch,
begin the cross stitching with the word 'Papa',
working outwards from the middle, using two
strands of thread in the needle. Complete the
embroidery and remove the tacking (basting)
stitches. Press on the wrong side.

⌐ MAKING THE BOOKMARK
Make a small double turning on the top edge,
folding the fabric to the wrong side; hem in place.

    To point the lower edge, fold the bookmark
lengthwise in half, right sides together. With
matching thread, backstitch across the short edge.
Press the seam open and turn to the right side.
Flatten out the bookmark to create the point, and
slipstitch to secure.

    Make the tassel by winding cream sewing
thread around a piece of card about 3 cm (1¼ in)
wide. Thread the loose end into a needle, slip the
tassel threads off the card and wind the loose
thread several times around one end. Pass the
needle up through the binding to emerge at the
top of the tassel. Sew onto the point of the
bookmark. Cut through the looped threads at the
bottom of the tassel.

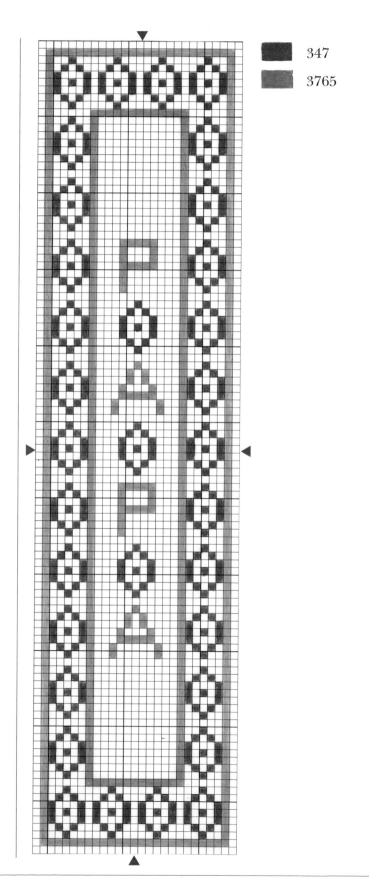

347

3765

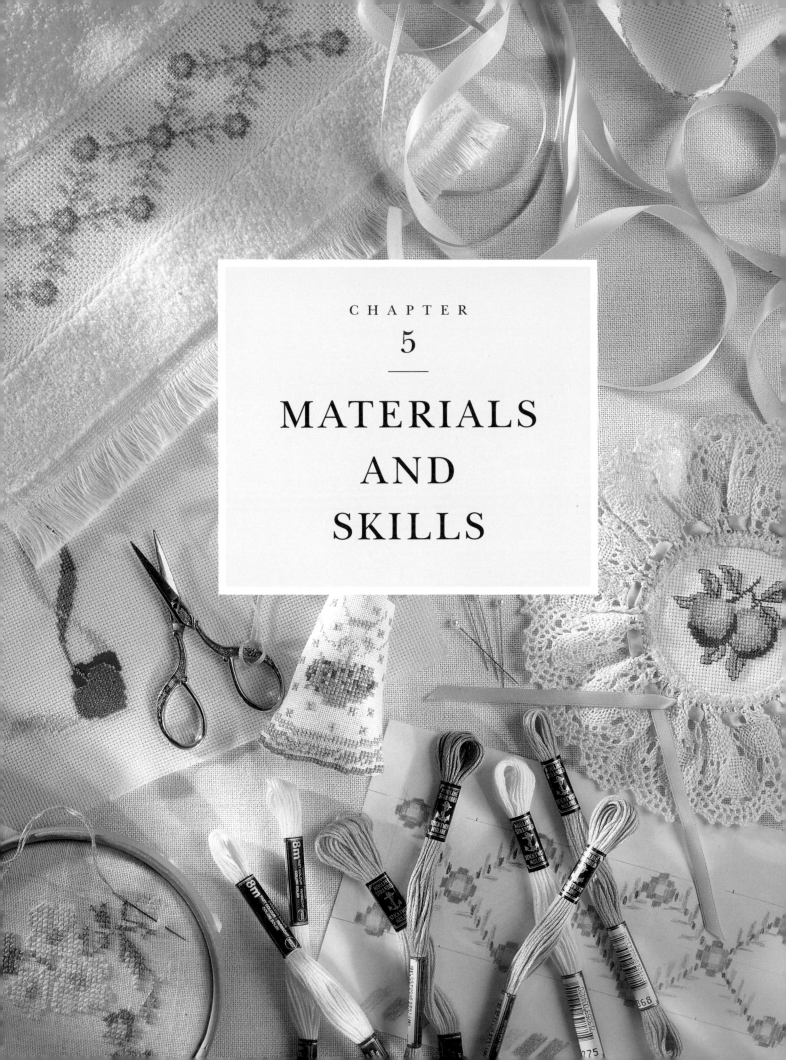

CHAPTER

5

—

MATERIALS
AND
SKILLS

⌐ FABRICS

Cross stitch embroidery is best worked on an evenweave fabric – that is, any fabric with the same number of threads counted in both directions, usually over 2.5 cm (1 in).

Linens are traditionally used for cross stitch embroidery around the world. They are available in a range of 'counts' and colors, although natural and antique finishes are more traditional. Some linens may have a pronounced uneven appearance – due to the staple (fiber) and nature of the flax from which it is woven – but this is what gives linen its distinguishing hand-made look.

Most linens are woven with a single weave with the exception of Hardanger, which has a double weave, and huckaback, which is woven in groups of threads (similar to cotton Aida) and forms a checked pattern.

In addition to linens, evenweave fabrics are also made from cotton and linen mixes, such as Zweigart's Quaker Cloth which comes in a limited range of colors and counts; pure cotton, such as Zweigart's Aida, Ainring, Lugana and Linda. These names signify the different counts and all these fabrics come in a variety of colors.

The finish given to these cotton fabrics may make them feel stiff and unyielding. On the one hand, the stiffness can help you to keep an even tension while stitching and will wash out with laundering but, on the other hand, you may prefer to hand-wash the fabric before starting.

⌐ THREADS

Embroidery threads: many types of embroidery thread can be used for cross stitch work, including pearl threads and *coton à broder*, but, for the projects given in this book, DMC six-stranded embroidery floss has been used throughout. The exact number of strands used for each project is given with the instructions.

As a rule, fewer strands are used on finer fabrics and more strands on heavier fabrics. The overall aim, however, is to produce clearly defined stitches that cover the fabric well.

Tacking (basting) thread: tacking (basting) thread is a soft, loosely twisted cotton which is normally sold on large reels, and is cheaper to use than ordinary sewing thread. The advantages of using tacking (basting) thread are that it will not leave a mark when it has been pressed with an iron, whereas ordinary sewing thread often does. Should it get caught up in any way while you are removing the stitches, it will break first rather than damage the fabric.

Sewing threads: these threads are tightly twisted, fine and yet strong. The most popular varieties are made from cotton or cotton/polyester mixes and come in a huge variety of colors, so matching a background fabric should not be difficult.

⌐ NEEDLES

Round-ended tapestry needles should be used for cross stitching on evenweave fabrics. You will find that they move easily between the fabric intersections without piercing the ground threads. Tapestry needles are available in sizes ranging from 18-26.

For making up the projects, you will also need a selection of sharps needles for hand sewing.

⌐ FRAMES

A hoop or rectangular frame will keep the fabric evenly stretched while stitching. While for smaller pieces of embroidery a frame is not essential, there are advantages to using one. When the fabric is supported in a frame, both hands are free to stitch – with one on top and one below, many people find they eventually stitch faster and more evenly this way.

⌐ SCISSORS

It is important to use the right type of scissors for the job. For cutting out fabric, use sharp, dressmaker's shears. You will need a pair of small, sharp-pointed embroidery scissors for snipping into seams and neatening threads, and for cutting cardboard, cords and paper, a pair of general-purpose scissors.

☞ SEWING MACHINE

A sewing machine is useful for making up items, especially for larger projects, where it will give a stronger seam and also help to speed up the finishing process.

☞ GENERAL ACCESSORIES

In addition to the above-mentioned items, you will need stainless steel pins, a long ruler and pencil, a tape measure, an iron and ironing board, and a thimble for hand sewing, especially through bulky seams.

☞ PREPARING THE FABRIC

Before cutting out, steam-press the fabric to remove all creases. Stubborn creases will be impossible to remove once they have been embroidered over so, if possible, avoid using that particular area of fabric. If colored fabrics are chosen for items you wish to launder, they should first be washed and pressed to test for colorfastness.

Always try to cut your fabric as economically as possible, placing pattern pieces as shown in the cutting layouts with individual projects to avoid wasting fabric.

Many evenweave fabrics, such as linen, fray very easily in the hand so, before you begin, it is a good idea to overcast the edges using tacking (basting) thread.

☞ WORKING IN A HOOP

The hoop is most popular for working relatively small areas of embroidery. A hoop consists of two rings, usually made from wood, which fit closely one inside the other. The outer ring has a screw attachment so that the tension of the fabric can be adjusted and held firmly in place while the fabric is embroidered.

Hoops are available in several sizes ranging from 10 cm (4 in) in diameter to very large quilting hoops measuring 60 cm (24 in) across. Hoops with table- or floor-stand attachments are also available.

1 To stretch your fabric in a hoop, place the area to be embroidered over the inner ring and press the outer ring over it with the tension screw released.

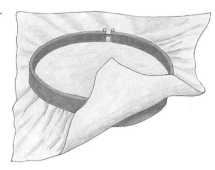

2 Smooth the fabric and straighten the grain before tightening the tension screw attachment. The fabric should be evenly stretched.

3 If desired, tissue paper can be placed between the outer ring and the embroidery, so that the hoop does not mark the fabric. Tear away the paper to reveal the fabric, as shown above.

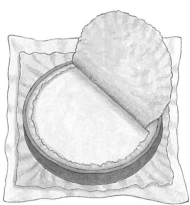

4 Alternatively, before stretching your fabric in the hoop, bind both rings with bias binding, essentially to stop the fabric from slipping (some fine linens can slip badly) and also to prevent the rings from leaving pressure marks.

☞ WORKING IN A RECTANGULAR FRAME

Rectangular frames are more popular for larger pieces of embroidery. They consist of two rollers with tapes attached, and two flat side pieces which slot into the rollers and are held in place by pegs or screw attachments.

These frames are measured by the length of the roller tape, and range in size from 30 cm (12 in) to 69 cm (27 in). They are also available with or without adjustable table- or floor-stands.

As an alternative to this kind of frame, canvas stretchers and old picture frames of an appropriate size can be used, and the fabric edges can simply be turned under and secured with drawing pins or staples.

1 To stretch your fabric in a rectangular frame, cut out the fabric, allowing at least an extra 5 cm (2 in) all around the finished size of the 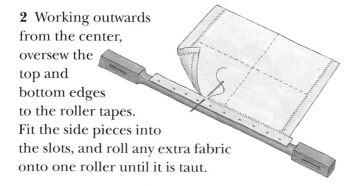 embroidery. Tack (baste) a single 12 mm (½ in) hem on the top and bottom edges, and oversew 2.5 cm (1 in) wide tape to the other two sides. Mark the center line both ways with tacking (basting) stitches.

2 Working outwards from the center, oversew the top and bottom edges to the roller tapes. Fit the side pieces into the slots, and roll any extra fabric onto one roller until it is taut.

3 Insert the pegs or adjust the screw attachments to secure the frame. Thread a large-eyed needle (chenille needle) with strong thread and lace both edges, securing the ends by winding them around the intersections of the frame. Lace the

webbing at 2.5 cm (1 in) intervals, stretching the fabric evenly.

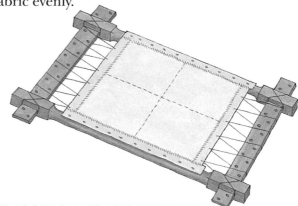

☞ ENLARGING A GRAPH PATTERN

There are one or two graph patterns given in the book which must first be enlarged to the correct size before you can use the pattern to cut out the fabric. The scale of the full-size pattern is given on the relevant page; for example, 'Each square = 5 cm (2 in)' means that each small square on the printed diagram corresponds to a 5 cm (2 in) square on your enlarged grid.

To enlarge a graph pattern, you will need a sheet of graph paper ruled in 1 cm (⅜ in) squares, a long ruler and pencil. If, for example, the scale is one square to 5 cm (2 in), 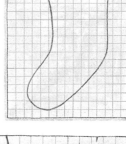 you should first mark the appropriate lines to give a grid of the correct size. Copy the graph freehand from the small grid to the larger one, completing one square at a time. Use the ruler to 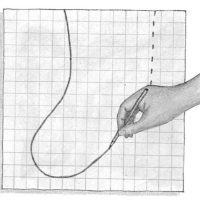 draw the straight lines first, and then copy the curves freehand. Transfer all construction points and instructions before cutting out.

✐ CROSS STITCH

The following two methods of working are used for all cross stitch embroidery. In each case, neat rows of stitches are produced on the wrong side of the fabric.

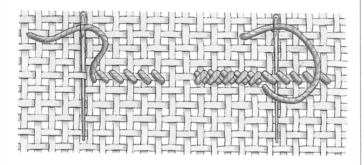

1 Work in horizontal rows when stitching large solid areas. Working from right to left, complete the first row of evenly spaced diagonal stitches over the specific number of threads given in the project instructions. Then, working from left to right, repeat the process. Continue in this way, making sure that each stitch and successive rows cross in the same direction throughout the piece of embroidery.

2 When stitching diagonal lines, or individual groups of stitches, work downwards, completing each stitch before moving to the next.

✐ BACKSTITCH

Backstitch is used in conjunction with cross stitch, sometimes for accompanying lettering but generally as an outline to emphasize a particular shape or shadow within a motif. The stitches are always worked over the same number of threads as the cross stitching to give uniformity to the finished embroidery. Use for continuous straight or diagonal lines.

Bring out the needle on the right side of the fabric and make the first stitch from left to right; pass the needle behind the fabric, and bring it out one stitch length ahead towards the left. Repeat and continue in this way along the stitchline.

✐ STITCHING BEADS

Bring out the needle in the appropriate place and thread on a bead. Insert the needle into the same hole, make a stitch underneath (the length of the bead) and bring it out with the thread below the needle. Take the needle through to the back just beyond where it last emerged, then bring it out ready to attach the next bead.

✐ TYING A QUILTING KNOT

1 Working on the wrong side, make one stitch through all layers leaving a long end. Make a second stitch at the same point.

2 Tie the ends together, right over left, left over right. Do not pull too tightly. Trim the loose ends to 12 mm (½ in).

TO MAKE A FRENCH KNOT

Bring the needle out where the knot is to be worked and, holding the thread down with the left thumb, wind the thread twice round the needle. Insert the needle close to the starting point and pull it through to the back of the embroidery so that a knot forms on the right side of the fabric, then fasten off the thread. If making more than one knot, don't fasten off; instead, reposition the needle for the next knot.

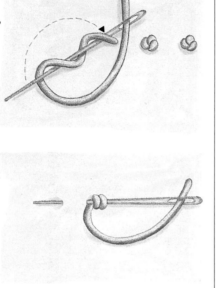

HEMMING STITCH

This small, almost invisible stitch can be used for all types of hems and for finishing edges which have been covered with a fabric binding, such as the Christmas Stockings.

Fold the hem or binding to the wrong side and pin or tack (baste) to secure. Using matching thread and holding the needle at an angle,

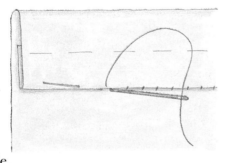

make a tiny stitch in the fabric first then insert it into the hem fold and make another small stitch. Pull the needle through and repeat along the stitchline, making the stitches of equal size and spacing them about 5 mm (³⁄₁₆ in) apart.

HEM-STITCH

This is a decorative way of turning up a hem and is the traditional stitch used on table linen and bed linen. For best results, hem-stitch should be worked on evenweave fabrics and fairly coarse weaves are the easiest to handle. Choose an embroidery thread similar in thickness to the fabric threads and use a tapestry needle to avoid piercing the fabric threads.

For a fringed finish, first remove a single thread at the hem and stitch along the line as shown. Complete the stitching and then remove the fabric threads below the hem-stitching to make the fringing.

To secure a hem that has been turned up to the drawn-thread line and tacked (basted) in place, work from the right side and hem-stitch as shown

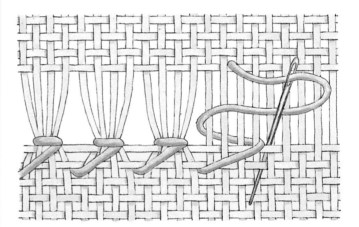

but, at the second stage of each stitch, make sure the needle pierces the hem at the back of the fabric before pulling the thread through ready to repeat the stitch along the line.

Bring the needle out on the right side of the fabric two threads below the drawn-thread line. Working from left to right, pick up either two or three threads, as shown in the diagram. Bring the needle out again and insert it behind the fabric, to emerge two threads down, ready to make the next stitch. Before reinserting the needle, pull the thread tight, so that the bound threads form a neat group.

Remember when hem-stitching Aida and other similar fabrics, that it is not necessary to remove the initial thread as the lines between the blocks of thread are clearly distinguished in the weaving. This means that the hem-stitching can easily be worked along a given line. As blocks and not single threads are being worked, make sure you refer to the project instructions for the number of blocks recommended for the hem-stitching.

☞ STRAIGHT SEAMS

Unless otherwise stated, all seams are straight seams with a 1 cm (⅜ in) seam allowance, pressed open to finish. In some cases, a French seam may be specified while others are neatened by machine zigzag stitching.

1 After stitching the seam, finish off the ends and steam-press the seam allowance to one side, to sink the stitches into the fabric.

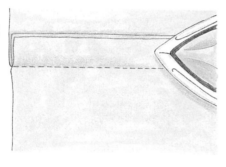

2 Press the seam allowances open, as shown. Remember to 'press as you sew' for best results when you are making up a project.

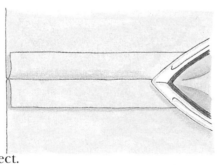

☞ FRENCH SEAM

A French seam is stitched twice, once from the right side and once from the wrong side. On light-weight fabrics, it looks best if the finished width is 6 mm (¼ in) or less.

1 With the wrong sides of the fabric together, stitch 1 cm (⅜ in) from the edge. Trim the seam allowance to 3 mm (⅛ in) and press the seam open.

2 Fold the right sides together, with the stitched line exactly on the folded edge, and press again. Stitch on the seamline, which is now 6 mm (¼ in) from the fold. Press the seam to one side.

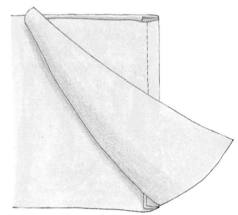

☞ PIPED SEAMS

Contrasting piping adds a decorative finish to a seam and looks particularly attractive on items such as cushion covers. You can enclose pre-shunk piping cord with either bias-cut fabric of your choice or with purchased bias binding. Alternatively precovered piping cord is available in several widths and many colors. Also available are specially-made cord pipings, see the Ring Pillow on page 43, which are applied in the same way.

1 To apply piping, pin and tack (baste) it to the right side of the fabric, with the seamlines matching. Clip into curved seam allowances where necessary.

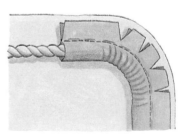

2 With the right sides together, place the second piece of fabric on top, enclosing the piping. Tack (baste) and then hand stitch in place. Alternatively, machine-stitch using the zipper foot. Stitch as close as possible to the piping, covering the first line of stitching.

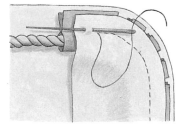

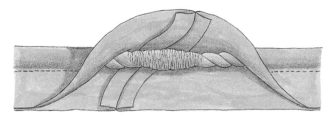

3 To join the ends of piping cord together, first overlap the two ends by about 2.5 cm (1 in). Undo the two cut ends of binding to reveal the cord. Join the binding strip as shown. Trim and press the seam open. Unravel and splice the two ends of cord, overstitching to secure them. Fold the bias binding over it, and finish stitching on the original stitchline.

⌒ BIAS BINDING

Bias binding is a narrow strip of fabric cut across the grain to allow maximum 'give', and is an excellent covering for all edges, especially curved ones. It is available in three sizes: 12 mm (½ in), 2.5 cm (1 in) and 5 cm (2 in), and in a wide range of colors. Cotton lawn is by far the most popular (and practical) type, and is stocked by most needlework suppliers.

These are two methods of binding an edge: one-stage binding, where the binding is attached by stitching through all layers, and two-stage binding, where it is attached in two stages so that the stitching cannot be seen on the right side.

For one-stage binding, using double-folded binding, encase the raw edge with binding and tack (baste) in place. Working from the right side, machine-stitch along the edge, through all layers, so that both sides are stitched at the same time.

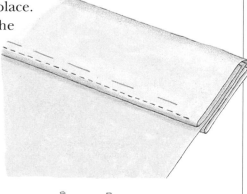

1 For two-stage binding, open out the fold on one edge of the binding and pin it in position on the fabric, right sides together, matching the foldline to the seamline. Fold over the cut end of the binding. Finish by overlapping the starting point by about 12 mm (½ in). Tack (baste) and machine-stitch along the seamline.

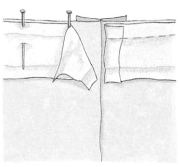

2 Fold the binding over the raw edge to the wrong side and tack (baste) in place. Then, using matching sewing thread, neatly hem to finish. Take the hemming stitches through the previously made stitches or place within the seam allowance to prevent them from showing on the right side.

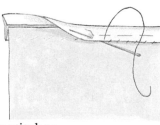

To join bias binding, cut the strips across the straight grain. Place them right sides together, pin and stitch across, and then press the seam open.

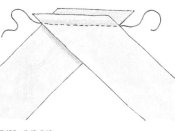

☞ ATTACHING A DECORATIVE CORD

To attach a fine- to medium-weight cord, simply slip one cut end into the seam – leave a 2 cm (¾ in) gap in the seam – and secure with matching thread. Slipstitch the cord around the edge of the cushion, alternately catching the underside of the cord and sliding the needle under a few threads of the seam so that the finished stitching is completely hidden. Finish with the two ends neatly tucked into the seam; cross them smoothly and secure with a few well-hidden stitches. Secure the seam opening in the same way.

☞ VERTICAL BUTTONHOLE

For a handmade buttonhole, first mark the position with pins, placing it centrally within the hem of the opening.

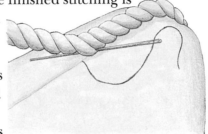

Using fine matching sewing thread, outline the shape of the buttonhole (a rectangle) with two rows of running stitches placed close together. Cut along the center through all layers. Check that the button will easily pass through.

Working from left to right, insert the needle from behind the slit with the point downwards, and bring it out just below the running stitches. Pass the thread around the point of the needle, from right to left, pull the needle through in the opposite direction to place the purl stitch on the cut edge.

Complete one side of the buttonhole and then take several threads across the end of the slit. Buttonhole over them to make a small strengthening bar. Repeat on the opposite side to finish on the wrong side of the fabric.

☞ MOUNTING EMBROIDERY

Embroidered pictures look best if they are first stretched over cardboard before framing under glass. A thin layer of wadding (batting) is placed between the fabric and the cardboard to give opaqueness and some protection to the corners and outer edges. Most fabrics used for cross stitch are fairly lightweight and can be attached at the back with pieces of masking tape, but heavier fabrics are best laced across the back with strong thread.

The cardboard should be cut to the size of the finished embroidery with, at least, an extra 6 mm (¼ in) added all around to allow for the recess in the picture frame.

Using a pencil, mark the center both ways on the cardboard. Mark the center of the wadding (batting) by placing pins in the middle of the outer edges. Lay the embroidery face down, center the wadding (batting) on top and then the cardboard, aligning pencil marks, pins and tacking (basting). Remove the pins.

1 To attach the fabric with masking tape, begin by folding over the fabric at each corner and securing it with small pieces of masking tape.

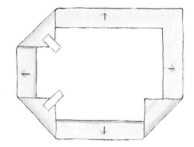

2 Working first on one side and then on the opposite side, fold over the fabric on all sides and secure it firmly with more pieces of masking tape, placed about 2.5 cm (1 in) apart. Check occasionally to see that the design is centered, and adjust the masking tape, if necessary. Neaten the mitered corners also with masking tape, pulling the fabric firmly to give a smooth even finish. Overstitch the mitered corners, if necessary.

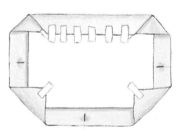

To attach the fabric by lacing, lay the embroidery face down with the wadding (batting) and cardboard centered on top, as shown in the

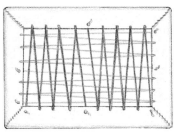

diagram. Begin with the corners, as shown, and also fold over the fabric on opposite sides, mitering the folds at the corners. Using strong thread knotted at one end and beginning in the middle of one side, lace across the two edges. Repeat on the other two sides. Finally, pull up the stitches fairly tightly to stretch the fabric evenly over the cardboard, periodically checking to see that your design is still centered. Adjust if necessary. Overstitch the mitered corners to finish.

ALPHABETS

Alphabets have always been a favorite subject for embroidery. Some of the most beautiful examples are those seen on traditional cross stitch samplers.

These were invariably practice pieces stitched by young girls as they learned to embroider. And as their skills improved, so the amount of lettering often increased. The samplers would then often include lengthy prose or verse imaginatively illustrated and arranged within colorful borders of flowers, fruit or other decorations.

The styles of alphabets and numerals suitable for cross stitch vary enormously and I have tried to reflect that variety using, for example, small letters backstitched in a single line for the Child's Prayer Sampler on page 19, larger cross-stitched words in mixed colors for the motto in the 'Welcome to my Kitchen' Sampler on page 87, and very decorative floral initials for the Baby's First Slippers on page 31.

As suggested in the project instructions, use the following alphabets to substitute the names and dates of your choice. For the Baby's Bonnet on page 28, for example, draw in your own name in the space provided on the graph, referring to the alphabet on page 156.

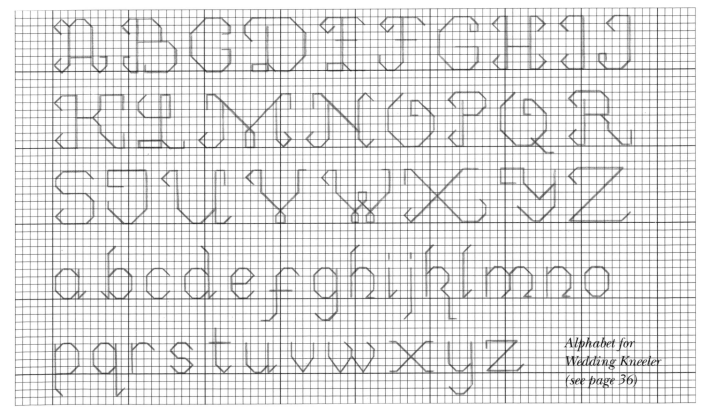

Alphabet for Wedding Kneeler (see page 36)

Alphabet for Baby's Crib Cover (see page 50)

Alphabet for Baby's First Slippers (see page 31)

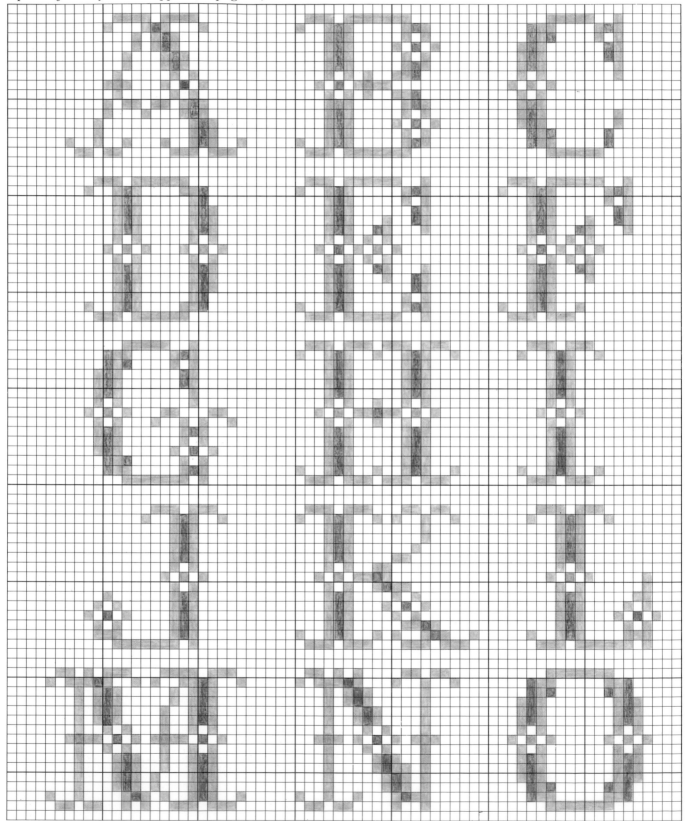

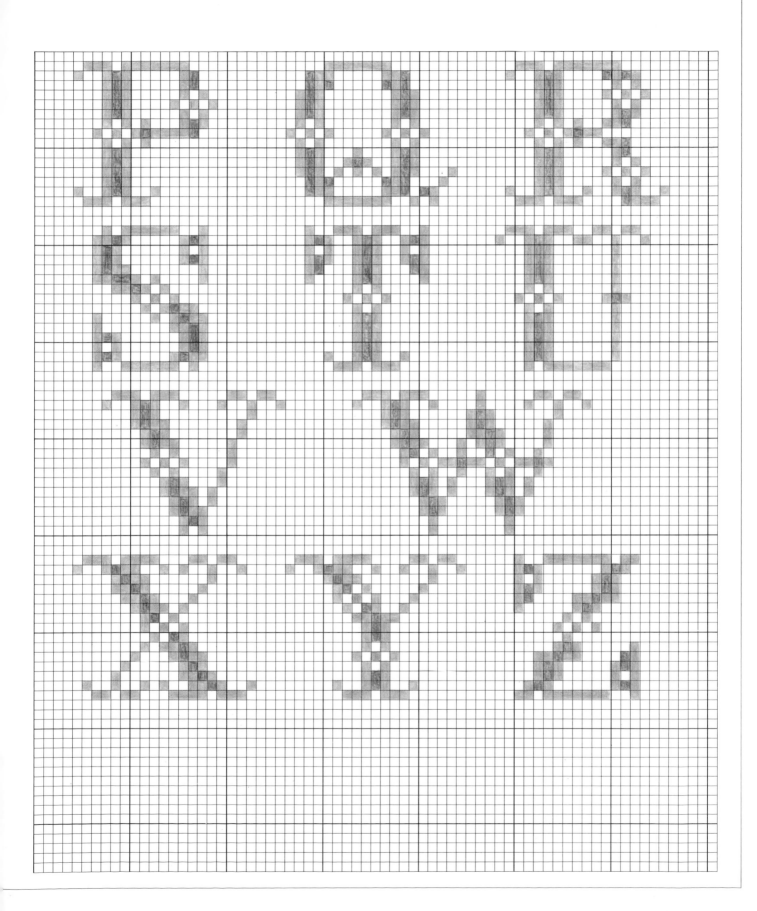

Alphabet for Ring Pillow (see page 43)

Alphabet for Baby's Bonnet (see page 28)

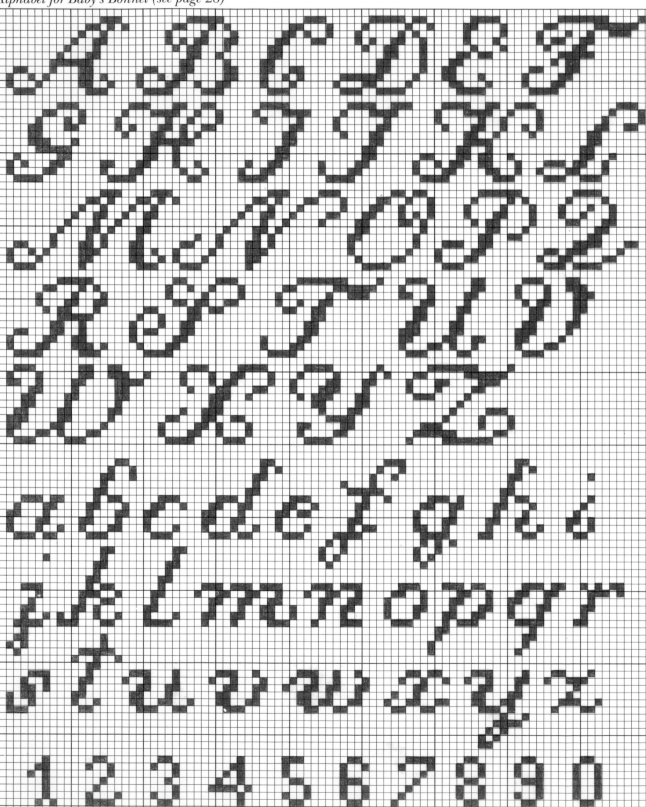

USEFUL ADDRESSES

I have used DMC threads and Zweigart fabrics throughout this book. These materials are available in many craft and fabric stores throughout North America. If you are unable to locate a supplier, contact the following addresses.

For information about DMC products:

DMC Corporation
10 Port Kearny
South Kearny, NJ 07032

To mail-order DMC products:

Herrschers
800/441-0838

For Zweigart products:

Needleworker's Delight
100 Claridge Place
Colonia, NJ 07067
800/931-4545

Presentation cards may be mail-ordered from:

Willmaur Crafts Corporation
735 Old York Road
Willow Grove, PA 19090
215/659-8702

Yarn Tree Designs, Inc.
P.O. Box 724
Ames, IA 50010
515/232-3121

BIBLIOGRAPHY

A Creative Guide to Cross Stitch Embroidery, Jan Eaton (New Holland, paperback 1993)

A Sampler of Alphabets (Sterling Publishing Co., 1987)

Around the World in Cross Stitch, Jan Eaton (New Holland, 1992)

The Cross Stitch and Sampler Book (Methuen, 1985)

Cross Stitch for Children, Dorothea Hall (Merehurst, 1992)

Cross Stitch for Special Occasions, Dorothea Hall (Merehurst, 1992)

Cross Stitch for the Home, Dorothea Hall (Merehurst, 1992)

Embroidery, Mary Gostelow (Marshall Cavendish Editions, 1977)

Embroidery Studio, The Embroiderers' Guild (David & Charles, 1993)

Fairy Tales in Cross Stitch (Merehurst, 1992)

Flowers in Cross Stitch, Shirley Watts (Merehurst, 1994)

Glorious Inspiration, Kaffe Fasset (Century, 1991)

Good Housekeeping Embroidery (1981)

Making Your Own Cross Stitch Gifts, Sheila Coulson (New Holland/Storey Publishing, 1994)

Nursery Rhymes in Cross Stitch (Merehurst, 1991)

Quick and Easy Cross Stitch, Dorothea Hall (Merehurst, 1992)

Traditional Samplers, Sarah Don (David & Charles, 1986)

Treasures from the Embroiderers' Guild Collection (David & Charles, 1991)

ACKNOWLEDGEMENTS

I would like to extend grateful thanks to the following people who have helped with cross stitching the designs, and who were always ready to share my enthusiasm with skill and understanding.

Caroline Davies

Christina Eustace

Janet Grey

Kerri Laver

Judith Maurer

Helen Milo

Julie Morgan

Janey Oak

Elena Thomas

Mary Walter

Anne Whitbourn

Thanks must also go to Cara Ackerman of DMC Creative World who helped in many ways, and supplied various evenweave fabrics and a selection of threads. Finally, to Alan Gray of Framecraft Miniatures Ltd who kindly supplied the lace-edged bookmark, the greeting card mounts and the preserve pot covers.

I NDEX

Cross stitch projects appear in bold type